Campaigning *With* Custer

D. L. SPOTTS
AT TIME OF ENLISTMENT

Campaigning With Custer

and the

Nineteenth Kansas Volunteer Cavalry

on the

Washita Campaign, 1868-'69

By DAVID L. SPOTTS

COMPRISING HIS DAILY DIARY OF THRILLING EVENTS ON
THE WINTER CAMPAIGN AGAINST THE HOSTILE
CHEYENNES, KIOWAS AND COMANCHES

Edited and Arranged for Publication
BY E. A. BRININSTOOL

University of Nebraska Press
Lincoln and London

Manufactured in the United States of America

First Bison Book printing: 1988
Most recent printing indicated by the first digit below:
1   2   3   4   5   6   7   8   9   10

Library of Congress Cataloging-in-Publication Data
Spotts, David L., b. 1848.
   Campaigning with Custer and the Nineteenth Kansas
Volunteer Cavalry on the Washita Campaign, 1868–69.
   Reprint. Originally published: Los Angeles, Calif.:
Wetzel Pub. Co., 1928.
   "Bison book."
   1. Spotts, David L., b. 1848. 2. Indians of North
America—Wars—1868–1869—Personal Narratives.
3. United States. Army. Kansas Cavalry Regiment,
19th (1868–1869) I. Brininstool, E. A. (Earl Alonzo),
1870–1957. II. Title.
E83.869.S76   1988   973.8′1′0924   87-30204
ISBN 0-8032-4176-3
ISBN 0-8032-9174-4 (pbk.)

Reprinted from the 1928 edition published by the Wetzel Publishing
Company, Los Angeles. For the Bison Book edition minor changes
have been made in the selection and placement of photographs.

CONTENTS

LIST OF ILLUSTRATIONS

Major-General Philip H. Sheridan

INTRODUCTORY

OTHING aroused the hostility of the Indians east of the Rockies more than the building of the Pacific railroads. They claimed that the engines would drive the buffaloes away and leave them without meat, even though they had ceded their lands to the Government for which they were to receive for all time, food, clothing and blankets for their families and enough guns and ammunition with which they could kill buffaloes and other game for their subsistence. They were also paid annuities yearly in cash, interest on the land ceded to the Government. They had made treaties to live at peace with their neighbors on the frontier. Agencies were established at all accessible points where forts were built and supplies kept for their use at all times. It is true that all these agents were in a position where they could not only be dishonest with the Government, but with the Indians also. For money, or other remuneration, traders were given the privilege of selling their goods to the Indians.

At certain times the old men, the women and children of the tribes came to the forts for their supplies of food and clothing and would camp for months to show they were peaceable, and at the same time the young warriors were a hundred or more miles away committing crimes by murdering the whites along the border. They were supplied with guns and ammunition by the agents of the Government and by traders which were used to kill and murder.

At first the workmen, graders, tracklayers and section men were driven off and many of them killed. Stage stations were attacked, the men killed and the horses taken.

Wagon trains going to the Colorado gold mines were attacked, the horses and mules stampeded, and women and children killed or wounded, or if captured, the goods destroyed and the wagons burned. The settlers were more shamefully treated than any, unless it was the soldiers. Three or four, or perhaps a half dozen warriors would ride up to a settler's cabin and would have no gun in sight. They would profess to be friends, if there were men present, and ask for something to eat. If this was complied with, they would wait until it was prepared and then the shooting would begin.

In a well-known instance, the husband and father was mortally wounded, the mother outraged in the presence of the dying husband and children. The oldest daughter was carried into a captivity worse than death. Many times the settlers' homes were captured and all the family killed and scalped, except in some instances the wife or daughter would be taken prisoner and the men who, perhaps were not at home, would get a few neighbors who had escaped and go in pursuit. They usually found their dead bodies at the first camping place, which plainly showed the horrible torture they endured before knife or tomahawk ended the innocent life.

All these crimes, and many more, were reported fully and promptly to the Army officers, who in turn reported them to the Government and asked for troops sufficient to punish the invaders for the heinous crimes which the Government was encouraging by feeding their families and issuing arms and ammunition to them. The Indian agents would report the Indians on their reservations and coming daily for their rations, and they had no knowledge of any trouble as reported by the Army.

Finally Governor Crawford of Kansas made a trip to Washington and entered a plea for protection for the settlers and likewise a plea for the officers of the Pacific rail-roads. A Peace Commission was sent to a Council with the tribes, instructed, if possible, to make a treaty of peace which would end the bloodshed and permit the building of the railroads. This was just what the Indians were glad to do, for they could, by a few promises, obtain a fresh supply of food, clothing, also blankets and plenty of ammunition with which to kill enough buffaloes for their winter meat supply. This was all the Peace Commission accomplished.

The Indians signed a treaty promising to be good if the Great Father at Washington would feed them well and allow them to hunt buffaloes in Western Kansas and give them plenty of guns and ammunition. Every tribe was represented by their principal chiefs and all promptly signed the treaty by their signature or cross. When this was accomplished they went back to their reservations apparently satisfied.

With the adjournment of the Peace Commission, the 18th Kansas Cavalry, which had been called out as volunteers to aid the U. S. troops to protect the settlers, were discharged and allowed to return to their homes.

Quiet reigned in Kansas until spring, when the grass appeared, and with it the buffaloes, which were closely followed by the Indians. It was soon manifest that these red demons had no idea of keeping their treaty. They immediately began repeating the crimes of the year before.

The Indians' supplies had reached Fort Harker and the Indians were there to receive them, but Gen. Sheridan, who had succeeded Gen. Harcock, forbade their being issued at that time. This created dissatisfaction as both the Indians and agents were demanding the distribution. Finally an order came from the Department of the Interior that the delivery be made. In a few days appeals came in to the Governor of Kansas for protection. First the Governor hastily raised a company of militia and went in person to assist where help seemed to be needed most, but many had already been killed. Then he sent the following dispatch to the President at Washington:

TOPEKA, KANSAS, AUGUST 17, 1868.

To His Excellency, Andrew Johnson, President:

I have just returned from Northwestern Kansas, the scene of a terrible Indian massacre. On the thirteenth and fourteenth instant, forty of our citizens were killed and wounded by the hostile Indians. Men, women and children were murdered indiscriminately. Many of them were scalped and their bodies mutilated. Women after receiving mortal wounds were outraged, and otherwise inhumanly treated in the presence of their dying husbands and children. Two young ladies and two little girls were carried away by the red-handed assassins, to suffer a fate worse than death. Houses were robbed and burned, and a large quantity of stock driven off.

The settlers, covering a space of sixty miles wide, and reaching from the Saline to the Republican, were driven in, the country laid in ashes and the soil drenched in blood. How long must we submit to such atrocities? Need we look to the Government for protection or must the people of Kansas protect themselves? If the Government cannot control these uncivilized barbarians, while they are under its fostering care and protection, it certainly can put a stop to the unbearable policy of supplying them with arms and ammunition, especially while they are waging war notoriously against frontier settlements, from the borders of Texas to the plains of Dakota. The savage devils have become intolerable, and must and shall be driven out of this State. Gen. Sheridan is doing and has done, all in his power to protect our people, but he is powerless for want of troops. If volunteers are needed, I will if desired, furnish the Government all that may be necessary to insure a permanent and lasting peace.

S. J. CRAWFORD, *Governor of Kansas.*

About all that came from the information given above was an order to Gen. Sherman to do all that was possible for the protection of the frontier—just what he was already doing.

On September 10 he sent Col. "Sandy" Forsyth of his staff, with Lieut. Beecher, Dr. Mooers and forty-seven scouts, all of whom were of dauntless courage and unerring aim, from Fort Wallace, in pursuit of a band of Cheyennes which had been committing depredations in that vicinity. They followed their trail for several days and on the 16th they encamped on Arickaree Creek near the northwestern corner of the State of Kansas. At the break of day the next morning a small party of Indians made a dash through Forsyth's camp and captured some of his horses. These were soon followed by the whole band of 800 or more, opening the fire in earnest.

The troops were obliged to leave their camp in the possession of the enemy and seek protection, while they had the opportunity. They took refuge on an island, or sand bar, in the creek and hastily made trenches and breastworks in the sand, from which they repulsed several charges made by the Indians, who left a considerable number of dead warriors behind.

Col. Forsyth was wounded at the first charge, but said nothing. Next two of his veteran scouts were killed and Lieut. Beecher and Dr. Mooers both mortally wounded. By night a large portion of their number was either killed or wounded, but they could see dead Indians piled on each other in their front.

With the approach of night the Indians withdrew, but placed a strong guard around the brave band to prevent their escape. Notwithstanding their caution it did not prevent two brave men from crawling through their lines. Jack Stillwell, a boy not yet 21, and Pete Trudeau, an old

French-Canadian trapper, slipped by the guards and made their way to Fort Wallace and notified Col. Bankhead. On the third night after the departure of Stillwell and Trudeau, Forsyth, not having heard from anyone, sent two more of the scouts, Capt. Allison J. Pliley and Jack Donovan, to Fort Wallace. On the second day out they met Col. Carpenter who was losing no time day or night to reach their comrades in distress. He was greeted with cheers and tears from those who were still living.

There were portions of several tribes represented in this fight and they paid dearly for whatever plunder they obtained. Roman Nose, a principal chief of the Cheyennes, and about seventy warriors were killed.

The Peace Commission again made an appeal to the Indians to go back to their reservations. They were not yet ready to go back as they had received arms and ammunition from the Government and also wanted more scalps, horses and other property. When they appeared on the plains in their war paint, ready to repeat their former offences, Gen. Sheridan was notified and he at once telegraphed Governor Crawford as follows:

FORT HAYS, KANSAS, OCT. 8TH, 1868.

Governor Crawford:

Gen. Hazen has informed me that the friendly overtures which were made to the Kiowas and Comanches at Larned, on the 19th and 20th of Sept., 1868, have failed to secure peace with them or remove them to their reservations. I am authorized to muster in one regiment of cavalry from your state for a period of six months. I will communicate further on the subject on receipt of additional instructions from Gen. Sherman.

P. H. SHERIDAN, *Maj. Gen., U. S. A.*

Gen. Sherman, being convinced the Peace Commission was both helpless and useless, lost all patience with the Indians and told Gen. Sheridan to proceed at once. On receipt of this authority the General telegraphed the Governor as follows:

HEADQUARTERS DEPARTMENT OF THE MISSOURI
IN THE FIELD, FORT HAYS, OCT. 9TH, 1868.

His Excellency, S. J. Crawford, Governor of Kansas:

Under directions received through Lieutenant General W. T. Sherman, commanding Military Division of the Missouri, from the Hon. Secretary of War, I am authorized to call on you for one regiment of mounted volunteers to serve for a period of six months, unless sooner discharged, against the hostile Indians on the plains. I therefore request that you furnish said regiment as speedily as possible to be rendezvoused and mustered into service of the United States at Topeka, Kansas.

The regiment to consist of one Colonel, three Majors, twelve Captains, twelve First Lieutenants, twelve Second Lieutenants, twelve companies of one hundred men each, including the required number of non-commissioned officers specified in the U. S. Army Regulations (1868), the pay, allowances, and emoluments of officers and men to be the same as that of U. S. Troops.

The men will be rationed from the time of their arrival at the rendezvous and will be furnished with arms, equipment, horses and clothing from the date of muster into the service of the U. S.

I have the honor to be, very respectfully,

Your Obedient Servant,

P. H. SHERIDAN, *Maj. Gen., U. S. A.*

On receipt of this despatch the call was issued at once and within twenty days a full regiment of 1200 men had assembled at Camp Crawford, a half mile below the city, and were being fully equipped for service on a winter campaign.

MAP OF THE 1868-69 CAMPAIGN OF THE 19TH KANSAS VOLUNTEER CAVALRY

OFFICERS OF
NINETEENTH KANSAS VOLUNTEER CAVALRY
1868

Colonel..Samuel J. Crawford
(Resigned February 12, 1869)
Colonel..Horace L. Moore
Lieutenant Colonel..Horace L. Moore
(Promoted to Colonel, March 23, 1869)
Major..William C. Jones
(Promoted to Lietenant Colonel, March 23, 1869)
Major..Charles Dimon
(Captain Company G., promoted to Major, March 23, 1869)
Major..Richard Jenkins
Major..Milton Stewart
(Captain Company K., promoted to Major March 23, 1869)
Surgeon..Mahlon Bailey
Assistant Surgeon..Ezra P. Russell
Assistant Surgeon..Robert Aikman
Adjutant..James W. Steele
Quartermaster..Luther A. Thresher
Commissary Subsistent..John Johnston
Sergeant Major..Geo. G. Gunning
Sergeant Major..John G. Kay
(Private Company K., promoted to Sergeant Major, April 4, 1869)
Quartermaster Sergeant......................................Francis M. Brown
(Private Company A., promoted)
Commissary Sergeant..William W. Mather
(Private Company A., promoted)
Hospital Steward..Gamaliel J. Lund
Chief Bugler..William Gruber
(Transferred from Company E., accidentally killed, March 6, 1869)
Chief Bugler..Enoch Collett
(Transferred from Company F.)
Veterinary Surgeon..George Davidson
(Transferred from Company A.)

COMMISSARY GUARD

Special detail to Commissary Department

Sergeant, John W. Casebier............................Company A
    Privates:
Lewis Harriman..Company A
Duncan McCarty..Company A
John Martin..Company B
George W. Warren..Company D
Benjamin F. Van Horn......................................Company D
Stephen J. Van Dorn..Company E
Andrew Gustaf..Company E
Augustus P. Ingleman......................................Company F
Wilson T. Sloan..Company H
Joseph W. Downing..Company I
George Vann..Company K
D. L. Spotts..Company L

15

Nineteenth Kansas Volunteer Cavalry
1868
COMPANY A.

Captain..Allison J. Pliley
First Lieutenant.................................Benjamin D. Wilson
Second Lieutenant...............................*Raleigh C. Powell
Second Lieutenant..Joseph Beacock
First Sergeant..James A. Hadley
Quartermaster Sergeant..............................Orrin A. Curtis

SERGEANTS

James W. Wilson   Lewis A. Howell   James M. Conwell
    Jeremiah McBee   John W. Casebier

CORPORALS

John Cooper	Ephraim B. Davis	Andrew J. Smith
William Sherman	Peter Cart	James P. McDowell
	Thomas E. Maddox	Bernard McMahon

Bugler: William G. Andrews

PRIVATES

Adams, William E.	Hudson, John H.	Perkins, Joseph D.
Alton, Olof	Jacobson, Andrew	Peterson, Soree N.
Brown, Francis M.	Johnson, Martin	Power, Stephen D.
Bryan, Frank E.	Johnson, Andrew P.	Razer, Guthart
Butler, Henry C.	James, Martin V.	Rice, William
Caldwell, James B.	Jordon, Sylvester	Riddle, Thomas
Canfield, Thomas P.	Laiblin, Charles F.	Rogers, Francis
Carleson, Charles	†Lorema, Joseph	Rogers, George W.
Cohee, Jefferson	Lazelle, Marmaduke D.	Searcy, Charles
Cooney, William	Linton, John	Shutts, Charles
Creek, Isaiah	Lundgren, Gustaf	Smith, George D.
Curtis, Noah E.	Maddox, John F.	Smith, William
Daubon, Frank E.	Maley, John	Stackhouse, Charles
Davidson, George	Menhall, Andrew J.	Stanley, James
Davis, William	Mason, William	Stumbaugh, Simpson
Dolloway, Charles C.	§Mather, William W.	Templeton, John C.
Duer, Thomas W.	Moffatt, Isaiah B.	Thompson, Archibald
Dunner, Albert	Morrison, John L.	Turner, John
Eckley, James	McBee, John	Updegraf, Albert
Enoch, Samuel	McClain, Willard	Vanderpool, Thomas B.
Fowler, Charles O.	McClain, James H.	Vane, Francis M.
Ferguson, Porter	McCarter, Reed	Walker, Livingston
Gay, William	McCarty, Duncan	Watkins, William
Hanson, John	McHazard, Cornelius	Williams, Francis M.
Hays, John M.	Nelson, Charles P.	Williams, Henry
Herriman, Lewis	Pappan, Stephen	Wright, Robert M.
Hilbish, Aaron	Pappan, Otevain	

*Resigned 1-5-'69. †Died. §Commissary Sergeant.

16

COMPANY B.

Captain..Charles E. Reck
First Lieutenant...............................Henry H. McCollister
Second Lieutenant...........................Charles H. Champney
First Sergeant.................................David P. Richards
Quartermaster................................William J. Wigg

SERGEANTS

John Rine   Adam Wilson   John Hill
     John W. Perry   Winfrey Mitchell

CORPORALS

Joseph Langlois   Patrick H. Donohoe   Jesse G. Lear
James R. Jupp   Joseph Rankle   Frank Sullivan
     Thomas Day   Charles Gardner

Farrier: George Abbott

PRIVATES

Albrecht, Frederick C.
Ammons, George
Angus, William
Bates, James L.
Bayliss, Theodore F.
Blakeley, Henry
Boen, John
Bradley, George H.
Bunshoe, Michael
Caruthers, William
Clites, Noah B.
Conger, Samuel
Connody, Arthur
Cox, Thomas
Craig, Dobson
Day, Dudley
Day, Allen
Deets, John W.
Deets, William
Dunkelberger, Nathan
Eaton, John
Epson, Polk
Estes, Asa
Falconer, James
Flynn, John W.
Fowler, Sidney
Gocher, Julius
Hann, William

Hardin, William J.
Harrell, Jacob
Harvey, Oliver H. P.
Horton, Charles W.
Hurst, Elisha S.
Jacobs, Peter
Jones, George M.
Jones, John M.
Judd, John M.
Key, William
Keplinger, Daniel S.
Lane, John W.
Langston, Jesse
Layton, Perry
Leonard, Peter
Letcher, Alexander
Letcher, William H.
Long, Elisha
Martin, John M.
Martin, Henry
Morris, Winfield S.
Morris, Jesse B.
McBride, William
Nelson, Samuel
Norris, Francis M.
Noyes, George
Parnell, George A.
Perkins, Nathan G.

Potter, George W.
Potter, Isaac
Potter, Daniel
Powell, Thomas
Reardon, Morris
Reed, James
Rhodes, Buford A.
Rutledge, Grandison
Runnells, Jestin
Schafer, Christian
Scott, Marion H.
Shanley, Thomas
Spencer, Josiah B.
Stewart, William
Stillwell, Wm. S.
Sturgeon, Alexander
Sweeney, William
Thompson, Andrew J.
Thompson, Levi S.
Thompson, Charles W.
Titus, Theodore
Turner, William H.
Walker, Michael
Warrine, Wm. H.
Watts, Joseph W.
Weathers, John H.
Woodford, Charles

17

COMPANY C.

Captain...Charles P. Twiss
First Lieutenant................................Walter J. Dallas
Second Lieutenant............................Jesse E. Parsons
First Sergeant................................Willington M. Friend
Quartermaster..................................Samuel J. Cowan

SERGEANTS

John McKenzie   Joseph Fanning   Jonathan A. Stoddard
Constantine G. Mull   Charles P. Smith

CORPORALS

John S. Peters   Duane D. Spicer   William E. Case
John B. Hamblin   George M. Longstreet   Adelbert E. Miller
William Givens   James McTye

Farrier: George A. Winans

PRIVATES

Adams, William
Allen, Reuben
Allen, William S.
Anderson, George T.
Bain, Benjamin F.
Barnett, Andrew
Baker, George
Becker, William F.
Bird, William
Black, James A.
Byfield, Marion J.
Caruthers, John
Castator, James L.
Castator, John P.
Christy, Francis M.
Christy, George W.
Clark, James M.
Clement, Charles A.
Clinton, William
Couchman, Samuel J.
Cooper, Josiah M.
Cox, John A.
Cress, Soloman P.
Denny, Isaiah
Denny, Columbus
Dow, George W.
Downs, William
Durland, Peter

Eltus, William S.
Evans, Charles J.
Fawcett, Franklin B.
Fitzpatrick, Jacob J.
Fitzsimmons, Robt. E.
Gilkeson, John S.
Gillihan, Lucius M.
Hall, David
Harrison, Alonzo M.
Hill, John A.
Hougham, Ira
Imel, Thomas J.
Inge, William
Jackson, Niton
Jamerson, Jasper
Jameyson, John E.
Johnson, Ebenezer
Johnson, Charles M.
Kimball, George A.
Kirpatrick, Crittenden
Kirpatrick, Clay
Lapham, Henry B.
Lawson, Emanuel
Lyon, William P.
Martin, William B.
Martin, Francis
Mix, Thomas L.
Moore, Richard P.

Moore, Emsley B.
McAfee, Albert
McDaniel, William B.
McKenzie, Joseph
McWilliams, Charles
O'Brien, Moses
Pierce, William M.
Pierce, John
Roush, Carey
Shamblin, Enoch
Simmons, Franklin F.
Smalley, Lyman O.
Spaur, Joseph G.
Swan, Davison R.
Taylor, Andrew J.
Thomas James H.
Van Slyke, Monroe
Vincent, George M.
Weiland, George M.
Wiggins, William
Willingham, William
Wilson, William F.
Wilson, Andrew
Wolford, Alfred T.
Woodin, John C.
Wyatt, Walter C.
Young, Julius

18

COMPANY D.

Captain	John Q. A. Norton
First Lieutenant	John S. Edie
Second Lieutenant	Charles H. Hoyt
First Sergeant	James R. Luckey
Quartermaster	Wm. H. Bartling

SERGEANTS

George A. Harris   James K. Titus   Alexander Mears
Argent Causdell   William D. Lesdenier

CORPORALS

William Hodson   William W. Whited   William Griffits
William F. Shaw   James F. Harris   Osmond Bayless
Elmer J. Kearns   Bruce Jones

Buglers: James Gearhart, Gabe McKenzie

PRIVATES

Adams, David
Adams, William J.
Ackerman, Daniel
Adolph, George
Ashford, William W.
Beardsley, George
Bess, Charles A.
Blake, John W.
Brander, Archie T.
Bressett, Sherman
Brooks, Jesse L.
Brown, Charles
Brunk, Daniel
Burket, Ransom
Cade, Benjamin
Carson, John M.
Crusan, William
Dally, Theodore
Davis, Harry H.
Davis, Josiah
Dickey, John
Elam, Tilman
Farrell, John H.
Fleck, Charles M.
Freelan, John B.
Fuller, James
Gilhousen, Hugo
Haines, Joshua

Hester, Joseph
Howell, Samuel
Hutchinson, Sylvester L.
Hymer, David F.
Jamison, Joshua
Lamb, James H.
Lane, William
Llewellyer, Robert
Lobinger, James C.
Long, James
Luckey, James R.
Marshall, William
Mewhinney, Mayo
Mitchell, George S.
Miler, Charles
Miller, Titus T.
Mix, Miles
McCormack, Jas. H.
Osborn, Robert
Owen, Robert B.
Persing, Aaron W.
Pole, William
Ports, Gideon W.
Ralston, Robert
Reser, Henry
Robinson, Francis M.
Rockey, William

Sanders, Charles N.
Schmucker, Chas. C.
Shank, Henry
Shaw, William F.
Simpson, Joseph B.
Smith, John
Smith, Alonzo M.
Stainbrook, James
Stafford, James H.
Supernaw, Jerry E.
Taylor, Noah V.
Van Horn, Ben F.
Walters, William
Warren, James R.
Warren, George W.
Warnicke, Andrew W.
Wells, Solon
Wells, David
Wheldon, Jeffrey H.
Whited, William R.
White, Edward F.
Williams, Henry
Williams, Oliver
Williams, James
Williamson, James F.
Williamson, Wm. T.
Wood, Benjamin

19

COMPANY E.

Captain	Thomas J. Darling
First Lieutenant	William B. Bidwell
Second Lieutenant	Charles T. Brady
First Sergeant	Geo. G. Gunning
First Sergeant	William Bernard
Quartermaster	Geo. B. Fortune

SERGEANTS

Harry J. Norris   James McBride   Joseph B. Henry
John Jaynes   George Price

CORPORALS

Early Harris   George Horr   Barnabas Welch
John Moore   Charles Calhoun   Martin Hendrickson
Eben L. Moulton

Buglers: Wm. Gruber (accidentally killed), William H. Lee

Saddler: Samuel Porter

Farriers: George Price, George W. Donaldson

PRIVATES

Allen, Charles E.	Goodman, David	Nelson, Marquis
Andrews, Homer A.	Greenlee, George W.	Nohlar, Jacob
Argo, Thomas	Griffin, Geo. W.	Norris, George
Armstrong, James	Griffin, George G.	Olvis, Samuel
Baker, James	Gustaf, Andrew	Porter, George W.
Bayless, Samuel M.	Havens, James	Powell, Charles
Bettinger, George	Hawkins, Jacob R.	Randall, Kimball S.
Biddle, Alfred	Herman, George	Rodgers, Warren
Blake, Charles H.	Hodshon, Richard	Sanders, Frank H.
Brophy, Thomas	Howe, Joseph P.	Shoeltzler, Jacob
Brown, Edward	Ingle, Isaac W.	Shaw, Charles S.
Burney, Christian	Johnson, Charles T.	Shirley, Robert N.
Clack, George	Jones, George W.	Simpson, George W.
Clifford, William B.	Lalley, James	Smith, Charles
Collins, Alonzo	Lawrence, Charles	Stafford, Robert B.
Critton, Jacob R.	Lee, James	Tomlinson, William
Davis, James	Leesman, Christopher	Tweedy, Thomas J.
Dreyfoos, Samuel	Lively, John R.	Van Dorn, Stephen J.
Day, John A.	Loss, Peter H.	Watson, John
Dobie, Adam N.	Melvin, Lewis	Weber, Frederick
Donaldson, Geo. W.	Millard, Jesse N.	Whithouse, George W.
Early, Elijah	Miller, Owen	Williams, Isaac
Fisher, John	Mitchell, Charles	Wainwright, Henry C.
Gentry, David	Mulready, John	Wolf, William H.
Gentry, Jesse	McGibbon, John	Winer, William
Gloory, Leopold	McMahon, James	Williams, Henry
	McGregor, Alexander	

20

COMPANY F.

Captain	George B. Jenness
First Lieutenant	DeWitt C. Jenness
Second Lieutenant	John Fellows
First Sergeant	John W. Ramsay
Quartermaster	Asdrubel Reed

SERGEANTS

James C. Wilson   Emmet Tallon   Edward Cassel
Gilbert Hickok

CORPORALS

Calvin T. Cottingham   Alexander Huddleston   Aldus D. L. Ross
Leander W. Taylor   John R. High   William Spire
Simon P. Hughes   Samuel H. McConnell

Buglers: Enoch Collett, Chief; John L. Rowton

Farrier: Joseph Miles

PRIVATES

Abrams, John
Abrams, Albert
Adams, John W.
Baird, Allan F.
Bingerman, Josephus
Blauch, David
Bledsoe, Samuel
Bringle, George L.
Bund, Allen F.
Burney, Daniel M.
Carter, Joshua
*Carpenter, Joseph
Cassel, Williams
Chapman, Zenas H.
Chase, John P.
Clark, William
Claypool, James C.
Collett, Isam
Crook, Thomas
Dale, Josephus H.
Dillen, George
Dillon, Jesse
Dunham, Wm. A.
Ealey, David
Emerson, David
Estes, DeWitt C.

Flack, Nicholas
Floyd, John P.
Gibbs, Francis M.
Green, Wing
Green, William L.
Hagen, Hugh
Hawley, Thomas L.
Holmes, Calvin
Howard, James M.
Howe, Gideon
Ingleman, Augustus P.
Johnson, Charles S.
Johnson, Henry
Johnson, Gilbert
Johnson, Thomas B.
Kimmil, W. T.
Kenney, John
Lawrence, John M.
Lighthiser, George W.
Loring, Williston
Mackey, James T.
Merritt, Thomas E.
Messenger, George G.
Miller, Geoge L.
Mitchell, Howard
McCord, William
McClure, Allen

McCullum, James
Noble, Clinton
Ogle, Charles
Pangburn, Alonzo
Perry, William
Peters, Henry
Quiggle, James G.
Quiggle, William
Rodgers, Phelps
Rowton, Joshua G.
Rhyner, William H.
Russell, James
Shaffer, James
Smith, Joel T.
Smith, William R.
Tabor, John H.
Tenbroock, James B.
Tilford, Alexander
Turle, John S.
Tinkelson, Frederick
Walker, Albert N.
Warner, Geo. W.
Wilder, Fred A.
Wise, Jeremiah
Wise, Robert H.
Wells, Joseph H.

*Transferred from Company I.

21

COMPANY G.

Captain..*Charles Dimon
Captain..†Richard Lander
First Lieutenant.................................Myron A. Wood
Second Lieutenant............................§Harry C. Letchfield
Second Lieutenant............................James W. Brown
First Sergeant..................................Leland Webb
Quartermaster..................................Thomas Maquire

SERGEANTS

Robert M. Cissna   Roland W. Curtin   William L. Wood
James Pluck   Ira B. Ogden

CORPORALS

Robert Howie	Francis W. Cook	Lucius S. Webb
Phillip G. Smilie	Thomas A. Roley	John H. Brown
John N. Martin	William M. Cook	Charles C. Bennett

Buglers: Moses M. Clinton, Antony Margraves

Farrier: Samuel Morris

Saddler: Edwin C. Smith

Blacksmith: William E. Wright

PRIVATES

Adkins, William	Gilreath, John W.	Perringer, Samuel W.
Armstrong, Ben C.	Greider, Robert	Pitman, John F.
Barney, James K.	Grooms, William	Ramsay, Thos. M. B.
Blair, Samuel A.	Janeway, Albert W.	Rayborn, William B.
Brown, James M.	Johnson, William S.	Reynolds, Thomas A.
Browne, Peres E. J.	Johnson, David	Rice, Joshua W.
Buffett, Oliver T.	Johnson, George H.	Richardson, Orange S.
Bugher, Stephen D.	Johnson, B. Augustus	‡Rodgers, John J.
Campbell, Martin L.	Jones, Harper	Roland, Peter
Card, Franklin J.	Kingsbury, David O.	Ross, Pleasant D.
Card, Barton J.	Lantis, Levi	Rucker, Elisha
Cissna, Mártin M.	Lee, Henry J.	Schwartz, Andrew
Connor, John A.	Loar, Burr T.	Segers, George
Connor, Willis A.	Lockerby, Abner P.	Smith, David
Cook, John W.	Lookinball, John F.	Smith, John W.
Coshow, Jacob	Melten, John T.	Sullivan, Dennis
Crum, Marcellus	Moore, John R.	Tack, William H.
Davis, John B.	McCoy, Francis	Tinlin, Alexander
Decker, Isaac R.	McMains, Andrew	Victor, Thomas A.
Dillon, Alfred	Oliver, John	Wiggs, William A.
Ficklin, Walter P.	Painter, William	Williams, John J.
Fundenberger, Wm. A.	Parkhurst, Elyah H.	Walfort, John
	Payne, Robert N.	

*Promoted to Major. †Promoted to Captain. §Resigned. ‡Died.

COMPANY H.

Captain..David L. Payne
First Lieutenant..Mount A. Gordon
Second Lieutenant..Robert M. Steele
First Sergeant..Charles H. West
Quartermaster..William W. Taylor

SERGEANTS

Stephen M. Hale   Julian C. White   Israel Broadsword
A. Chester Watrous   Wm. P. Floyd

CORPORALS

Harry Green   Harry E. Courtney   William Miller
Augustus Englebrick   Charles Kelsey   James M. Courtney
Jackson A. Neff

Buglers: Philip Grebling, Morgan Wright

Farrier: Andrew Weyer

PRIVATES

Abbott, Charles
Adams, Joshua T.
Alexander, George W.
Archer, William H.
Bailey, James M.
Baker, David
Berry, James S.
Bill, Marshall W.
Bickle, Charles F.
Blawser, Samuel
Bohrer, Mordecai
Bonesteel, Maxon
Boothe, Harvey
Brackett, Wesley
Brooks, William
Broomfield, James
Burnett, Theopholes
Chamberlain, Ira
Chase, James H.
Cherry, George L.
Childers, John
Clarke, John W.
Clayborne, Shelby
Conklin, George W.
Cox, William
Dannevick, Peter
Fee, John

Fleming, James
Foster, Charles
Freeman, Emsley
Gardwood, Wilberforce
Gokey, Charles
Gordon, John J.
Green, Franklin
Gruber, Martin
Hall, Howard H.
Harlan, William H.
Henderson, William P.
Herman, John
Huddleson, Robert C.
Huyck, Lewis C.
Jenkins, George S.
Johnson, Benjamin F.
Johnson, Thomas H.
Kelsey, Charles
Keneday, Charles
Landers, William
Law, Wilson A.
Linton, Thomas S.
Marango, Charles
Meek, John B.
Meek, Joseph W.
Miller, Lemuel
Moore, Charles
Monson, Thomas A.

McCarty, John
McCarty, Jerry
McIntire, Valorus
McNickle, John
Nites, Edward
Phillips, Charles
Pike, William
Piper, George B.
Porter, Mathew
Raymond, Harry B.
Rhodes, James H.
Rhodes, William
Ryan, John
Scott, William W.
Seman, Columbia A.
Shull, Cyrus
Sloan, Wilson T.
Strange, William H.
Stewart, William F.
Vasser, Samuel J.
Vancuren, Alva H.
Waters, Thomas
Watrous, James H.
Wells, John
Woodworth, James W.
Young, Elisha
Young, William

23

COMPANY I.

Captain..Roger A. Ellsworth
First Lieutenant................................James J. Clancy
Second Lieutenant...........................James M. May
First Sergeant.................................William H. Wilson
Quartermaster...................................Jacob Durand

SERGEANTS

Joseph II. Wilhite William H. Peers Wm. D. Hamilton

CORPORALS

Jesse S. Spencer James Townsley Charles Hunter
Milton J. Speerlock Nicolas Peterson

Bugler: Asa R. Bishop

PRIVATES

Adams, Merrett
Adkins, Taylor
Banks, Joseph
Bair, John L.
Bayse, Richard
Beall, Oliver M.
Belt, Osborne W.
Berry, Elias
Bevin, John F.
Bryant, Albert M.
Carpenter, Joseph H.
Calkins, Hubert
Conwell, Rolla H.
Cook, Thomas E.
Cooper, Arthur B.
Dale, William L.
Dailey, John M.
Deatley, George W.
Dowler, Charles
Downing, Joseph W.
Dykes, Francis M.
Egan, Michal W.
English, George
Eshom, Leonard M.
Faler, Daniel P.
Field, Isaac
Finn, Edward
Fightner, John
Fitzgerald, Wm. M.

Fletcher, Thos. M.
Gilmore, Mathies
Guise, John R.
Hinton, John
Horn, William
Holden, Wm. R.
Hull, Joseph S.
Imel, Thomas
Jewel, Cress
Johnson, Robert
Leach, James
Leathers, John
Lowery, Thomas M.
Maphet, John R.
Maphet, Charles W.
Marcy, Mortimer K.
Mead, Norman
Meats, A. Francis
Means, A.
Merritt, John R.
Millhouse, Isaac
Murphy, Edwards
McCoy, Isaac
McCumber, Harry D.
McDow, John F.
McLean, William F.
McKnight, Thos. N.
McGue, William K.
Nelson, Clark

Odiorne, Milton
O'Neil, Jasper
Orwig, Anson J.
Perrott, Benjamin F.
Pearson, Henry
Pittman, Aradia M.
Pool, John
Ramsay, Daniel W.
Reynolds, Walter S.
Roberts, Charles
Rutledge, Dudley
Shultz, Odellon B.
Smith, Charles
Stanfield, Alexander
Stansbury, Benj. F.
Stone, John S.
Street, William D.
Studebaker, Wm. F.
Thomas, Cassius E.
Tull, James M.
Tyler, John
Wardell, Levi
Warren, Thomas
Waterman, Bruce
Wilfer, Edward
White, Charles
Whipps, Robert
Wilson, Charles F.
Wright, William C.

24

COMPANY K.

Captain	*Milton Stewart
Captain	Emmet Ryus
First Lieutenant	Charles H. Hallett
Second Lieutenant	Robert I. Sharp
First Sergeant	Martin L. Stultz
First Sergeant	Arthur S. Pierce
Quartermaster	West B. Converse

SERGEANTS

George W. Lawrence	†John G. Kay	Charles E. Pierpont
Martin L. Stultz	John H. Adams	Wm. F. Converse

CORPORALS

Edward Bell	Orlando Soward	Wm. W. Graves
Wesley Kress	Albert B. Morse	Daniel Mack
	Mike Hyner	

Buglers: James N. Powell, Theodore Dodge

Farrier: Charles Brown

PRIVATES

Armstrong, Charles	Freeman, William C.	McNeal, John
Baker, William	Freeman, Andrew J.	Norton, Edley H.
Barnes, Lewis V.	Freeman, Calvin H.	O'Brien, Patrick
Basseler, Simon Z.	Gardner, Thomas H.	O'Connor, Joseph
Beedle, Martin B.	Garrett, Andrew	Paine, John
Black, William O.	Garrett, Jacob	Powell, Robert
Boone, Daniel	Graves, Wm. W.	Pruett, Thomas
Brensaw, Lewis	Gregory, Albert	Pullen, Woodford
Brown, Charles H.	Hamilton, Samuel	Robinson, Geo.
Bulton, Frank	Hennessey, Joseph	Rose, Geo. W.
Byarlay, Samuel A.	Herrigan, Mike	Rosenberger, John A.
Cagle, William	Hogue, Charles	Ryan, Stephen
Carroll, Henry S.	Holmes, Harvey	Salm, Frank W.
Campbell, James	James, Charles W.	Scott, Madison M.
Cesseriske, John	Kersey, Henry	Sercey, George W.
Chase, Robert	Kersey, John G.	Sharp, Milton
Chase, Aaron G.	King, Thomas A.	Shidler, Riley
Collins, John	Kuddlebeck, Wm. R.	Smithey, Lewis
Converse, Wm. F.	Lotham, Geo. F.	Spicer, Elijah
Cunningham, John W.	Marshall, Watson	Sweeney, Sol. L.
Davis, John	Mead, Benjamin	Vann, Geo. W.
Drake, DeMortimer	Meeker, Thaddeus	Wadsten, Frederick
Dyer, William H.	Miller, Robert C.	Watson, James A.
Eagen, James	Miller, Peter H.	Wesseler, Henry
Easton, James	Moon, Stover	Walker, John M.
Engle, Charles B.	McBolton, John	Winnerstrom, Hugo
Eppers, Julius	McFarland, Jas. W.	Yates, Jackson

*Promoted to Major. †Promoted Sergt. Major.

COMPANY L.

Captain..Charles H. Finch
First Lieutenant................................Henry E. Stoddard
Second Lieutenant.............................Winfield S. Tilton
First Sergeant....................................Charles Streight
Quartermaster....................................Thomas D. DeLong

SERGEANTS

Joseph B. Boothe   *David Dougherty   Andrew J. Maiden
John W. Lowe   Samuel F. Miller

CORPORALS

John L. Estes   John R. Atwood   John Burch
Thomas B. Carr

Buglers: Adam Davis, Rolla R. Watt

Farrier: John Gleason

PRIVATES

Adams, Frank
Anderson, James
Burgess, Benj. P.
Campbell, Cyrus
Carroll, Jeremiah
Cole, John M.
Contra, Thomas
Crawford, John C.
Daniel, Nathan T.
DeHart, George
Despard, Frank
Dodson, Foreman M.
Doughty, William F.
Elder, Ike S.
Epson, John
Fenner, Samuel S.
Filtenburger, John
Francis, William
Froman, Wm. J. Jr.
Gaddy, Richard M.
Gibson, William
Gile, Henry
Haines, Charles H.
Huddleson, William
Henderson, Aug. W.
Hills, David T.
Howard, James
Imel, James M.

Jewell, John W.
Johnson, Thomas
King, Luther C.
Kitchen, Edw. L.
Kitchen, David T.
Lamb, Hiram
LaFountaine, Amos
Lee, Oscar O.
Lowry, Edward
Lykins, Edward W.
Mahr, Frederick
Mann, Joseph T.
Manwell, George W.
Marks, William J.
Milne, James G.
Moreland, Joseph
Merriss, William W.
Murray, Solomon
McCall, Thomas
McCleary, Robert
McCarty, Frank
Mills, William
Millis, Charles D.
McIntosh, Sylvester
Odell, Adam C.
Ott, Robert
Parsons, Orlando
Patton, John D.

Phenix, Peter J.
Pierce, Russell H.
Pinnegar, Wm. H.
Porter, John
Pratt, Kossuth
Radenbocker, Wm. J.
Ravenscraft, John
Rayhill, Mathew
Riley, James N.
Rodgers, Jesse
Roney, Thomas B.
Shiverdaker, Perry
Shriver, Samuel
†Sibbitt, William
Sinclair, Sanford
Smith, Alfred F.
Smith, Thomas
Sparks, Sylvester
Spotts, David L.
Studabecker, John
Teas, Lewis
Ware, John F.
Warren, Thos. F
Webb, Alfred H.
Webber, Joshua
Wheeler, Samuel
Wolf, William
Wood, Alfred N.

*Promoted from Corporal.   †Died.

26

COMPANY M.

Captain..Sargent Moody
First Lieutenant.....................................James Graham
Second Lieutenant...............................James P. Hurst
First Sergeant.......................................James P. Wilson
Quartermaster......................................James H. Dunagan

SERGEANTS

George W. Waddle   Major A. Victor   Frank Johnson
George Tarbell   Richard O'Rourke   *Frank J. Burleigh

CORPORALS

Charles Scott   James Rose   Jacob Sutter
Irwin Rodgers   Charles Pollard   Henry Williams
Lorraine Bernard   John Marsh   George Darnell

Buglers: Frederick Grew, Frederick J. Merritt

Farrier: Henry Smith

PRIVATES

Aldrich, Oliver W.	Gibbons, John	Musgrave, Asa
Allen, Moses	Gibbs, Charles P.	Myers, Jonathan
Arnold, Eli J.	Gibson, George	McCullough, Moses
Bagley, Lorenzo	Gill, William H.	Norton, David
Baird, James	Grew, Frederick	Parker, John
Baker, Charles	Griner, Samuel G.	Paulley, James
Baldwin, Edward B.	Gray, Newton	Phenis, Charles
Blake, Bernesley E.	Hardin, Daniel K.	Platts, James
Bowen, Myron	Hensley, Abraham	Priddy, Charles
Boyer, George	Herrington, Jas. W.	Quackenbush, James
Brennan, John	Hester, William	Runyan, Alfred L.
Bryant, Henderson N.	Holloway, Lindsley	Samona, Julian
Chalender, William	Huber, Joseph	Sands, Alfred
Clark, George	Jennings, Francis	Smith, Alonzo
Colvin, Isaac	Johnson, Frank	Smith, Eben C.
Cox, John	Johnson, Thos. R.	Snyder, Francis N.
Dale, Georges	Kelley, James C.	Stillson, James
Davis, Leonidas L.	Kendall, Edwin N.	Stubbs, Alfred A.
Denmire, Theodore	Kennedy, Royal	Thomas, Henry
Denny, James N.	King, Levi, Jr.	Tierney, Thomas
DeWitt, Charles	Lake, Seth	Vandercase, Henry N.
Diehl, Philip	Matney, James	Van Vliet, Luther
Dobson, Joseph	Mattey, William	Vicar, James
Ehl, Frank	Mestes, Sioux	Vonwell, John
Elliott, John	Mitchell, William	Watson, John C.
Fielder, Comodore	Moore, John C.	Wheney, Holland G.
Gaun, William W.	Moses, James W.	Yawning, Garrett

*Promoted from Corporal.

27

SAMUEL J. CRAWFORD, GOVERNOR OF
KANSAS, AS COLONEL OF THE 19TH
KANSAS VOLUNTEER CAVALRY

From "Kansas in the '60s"

PREFACE

Y HOME was in Logansport, Indiana, where I had finished High School and wanted to see what there was for me in the future. When an opportunity came for me to drive a team to Kansas for Benjamin Gibson, who was moving his family to that State, I gladly accepted the offer.

We left Logansport on the 7th of June and arrived at Olathe, Kansas, on July 18, 1868. After calling on some of my friends, formerly of Indiana, I went to Springhill, nine miles south of Olathe, on the highway to Fort Scott. Here I visited the family of Wm. Corbett, a former neighbor in the East.

I had intended to go out on the frontier and take up a claim of 160 acres, but learned that it was extremely hazardous at this time, for the Indians were killing the settlers and the army was unable to keep them on the reservations. For a year or more the tribes, both north and south, had been making raids on small bodies of troops at every opportunity and usually all were killed.

Stage stations were destroyed, emigrant trains attacked and horses stampeded. They also made raids upon the frontier settlers, killing the men, destroying their property and carrying the women into captivity where they were held in abject slavery or met a horrible death.

After visiting the Corbetts I concluded to find employment until it was safe to go farther west and locate a claim. Through the recommendation of Mr. Corbett I obtained a position with Hiram Mitchell, a cattle man. My work was that of a "rustler" or anything that presented itself. But I soon had more responsibility given me. My object was to at least make expenses.

Springhill was a town of 200 or 300 inhabitants on the west side of the highway between Olathe and Paola in Johnson County, Kansas.

The town was one half mile square in the center of which was a public park, one block, planted to lawn and ornamental trees. The business houses nearly all faced the park. They consisted of a hotel, a general merchandise store and other smaller stores. Nearly every business was represented.

Mr. Corbett's farm was across the highway, east of town, and Mr. Mitchell's farm north of Mr. Corbett's and one-quarter of a mile from town. In Mr. Mitchell's family were his wife, two boys, Lewis and John, and a little girl named Eva. There were others staying there: Rufus Mitchell, a brother, Charles H. Finch, a cattle buyer for Mitchell, and Ned Stoddard, a recruiting officer who was making his headquarters there, as he was trying to raise a company of cavalry to assist Kansas.

The Secretary of War had called on the Governor of Kansas for a regiment of cavalry to assist Gen. Custer to drive the hostile Indians on their reservations. Stoddard was very anxious that I should enlist. It was my opportunity to help make the frontier safe for settlers and I perhaps could find the quarter section that would fulfill my expectations, so I was seriously considering the matter. I would not be 21 years old until the following February 15, and the call was for men 21 years old and under 35, so I was not sure that they would accept me. Finch and I were now pretty good friends and I liked him very much and if he enlisted I thought I would, also. Stoddard was very anxious that we give him our signatures as he had not been able to secure more than half a dozen names. If I went I determined to keep a diary of my experience.

D. L. SPOTTS.

DIARY OF D. L. SPOTTS

Thursday, October 15, 1868

Mr. Mitchell has a good many cattle on a range several miles away and this place of 320 acres is planted to corn. He brings part of the herd here and feeds them corn for the market. He is digging a big stock well, eight feet in diameter and has hired a couple of negroes to do the work. My part in the work is to see that their tools are kept in order and do other things that are necessary about the place.

Stoddard and Finch have agreed to go recruiting together tomorrow. Stoddard is not very well known and Finch knows nearly every one in this part of the country. They hope to have better success. I have agreed to enlist if they will omit the oath that I am 21 years old. They said while I was so near they would take me, as a couple of months would not make any difference, so I signed the roll and have agreed to become a U. S. cavalryman. There were less than a dozen names on the list and Stoddard has been over a week securing that many. We are supposed to be in the field by the 1st.

Friday, October 16, 1868

They have struck a big rock in the well that extends half the way across. I had to get dynamite and powder so it could be blasted. The negroes are afraid to use it, but I had them drill holes for blasting. We hear today that a new railroad is soon to be built through here from Olathe to Fort Scott and the surveyors are coming this way from Olathe.

I am very much interested in the trip I am soon to take to the frontier. Ten days is the limit in which the regiment is to be completed and mustered into the service. When the officers came in tonight they had secured nearly a dozen who had agreed to go. A good many more are anxious to go, but have private interests which prohibit their going on such short notice. Stoddard says Charlie is surely a hustler as nearly everyone he talks to is anxious to go.

Saturday, October 17, 1868

The officers started out early this morning. We did not work on the well today. Mr. Mitchell says he will get a man to blast out the rock, in a day or two. He has bought a big steer that weighs over 2100 pounds and is so poor we could count his ribs 100 feet away. It is the largest steer I ever saw. I helped haul a load of pumpkins for him, until the corn got riper. He can eat nearly a half load of pumpkins at one feed.

I heard tonight the railroad surveyors were within a mile of town and were on the east side of the highway which would probably bring the new railroad through the Mitchell place. It was good news when the recruiting officers came in tonight and reported fourteen more names who were ready and anxious to go, besides there were more who are good prospects. A man called today to see the recruiting officers. He said his name was Roberts and was a recruiting officer in Olathe. He left word for Stoddard to come and see him.

Sunday, October 18, 1868

After breakfast we go over to town and meet people as they come in from the country. The excitement is growing all the time. Three boys whom I have met, and who live here, have enlisted. Their names are: John Haigler, John Estes and Newton Riley. After lunch, Stoddard went to Olathe to see Roberts, who has over twenty names on his list and has as many more in prospect. Finch is out among the boys all day and they tell him they would put their names down if he was to be captain. My friend John Corbett says he would like to go, but he could not leave his business so soon. There are many others having interests which keep them at home. Men who have families are as enthusiastic as the rest and many would go if they could get away.

Monday, October 19, 1868

Stoddard and Finch went up in the north part of the county today and at Shawneetown they met a man named Ike S. Elder who had recruited several men and they were going up to Topeka to enlist, but have agreed to join the company enrolled in this county, after he was assured the boys would try and get him a good non-commissioned office in the company. The officers came back to Springhill through the western part of the county and found the excitement had become so general that many were ready to go, but would not sign the roll until they knew who were to be their officers. That seems to be the objection to enlistment now. They want to know before they sign the roll who are likely to be their officers so they can learn something about them.

Now none are asked to sign the roll, but have been given the names of Stoddard, Roberts and Finch as those most likely to be selected, so the men can look up their records and make selections. We have done nothing at the well today and have seen nothing of the surveyors.

I went over to town tonight and attended a meeting for the recruits. We hear a lot of Army talk and everyone is so greatly enthused that you might think a whole company could be raised in Springhill.

Tuesday, October 20, 1868

The recruiting officers had a meeting in Olathe today and received orders from Topeka that if they were not there by the 27th they were likely to be too late; for recruits were coming in very fast. They decided to notify the men who were likely to go, to be ready by Monday. Couriers were to be sent to all parts of the county to notify them to meet in Olathe on Monday, October 26, at 10 o'clock, when they would proceed to DeSoto and take the train.

There are now sixty-three who have signed the roll and twice as many who have agreed to go if they can be ready by that time. It is thought a full company can be raised in Johnson County. Meetings are to be held at several places in the county on Saturday evening and arrangements made for transportation to the train. We meet nearly every night over at the school house and some of the young fellows are pretty good recruiting officers.

Wednesday, October 21, 1868

It looks very much like rain all day, but the officers have gone to make arrangements for the meetings next Saturday evening and to notify the men, who are likely to go, to be there; also, those who can furnish teams to take them. Two boys from Missouri came today and wanted to enlist. Mrs. Mitchell asked them to dinner. One of them is a German, quite comical and his talk greatly amused the Mitchell boys. He told them they were going to join the Army and when the Indians saw Frank Doty and Bill Radenbocker coming they would lose no time getting back

GEN. GEORGE A. CUSTER.
THE LAST PHOTOGRAPH TAKEN OF THE GENERAL.

on their reservations. They asked me to give them something to do and I kept them pretty busy all afternoon.

As soon as one of the officers returned they both signed the roll. Mrs. Mitchell told them they could help for their board until ready to go on Monday morning. Both are good workers and my month is up so we are working to pay expenses.

Thursday, October 22, 1868

The three of us work together today and get pretty well acquainted. We cannot talk much else except about our trip. We are anxious to get on the frontier where we can have some excitement. We want to see Gen. Custer and his 7th Cavalry that we hear we are to join somewhere in the Indian country.

Bill says when Custer sees him he will put him in the front where the Indians can see him and they will be so scared the cavalry can ride up and take them, and save all the ammunition. The officers have been in the eastern part of the county today, making arrangements for meetings. They are also getting better acquainted with the boys whom they expect to command and the boys will be better able to decide on the men they want for commanding officers.

I understand the men will have the opportunity to vote for captain and the two lieutenants, but this will not take place until they are all together in the camp at Topeka, just before we are mustered into the service.

Friday, October 23, 1868

The railroad surveyors have run their line through the Mitchell farm today and the stakes are less than 100 feet from the big well that is being dug. Mr. Mitchell has stopped work on it, until the railroad is finally located, as it is too close to the present line.

Between the Army and the railroad, Springhill is a pretty lively town just now. The business men are holding meetings to decide where they want the depot and the young men have a meeting to see how many are going to join the Army. Several came over from the surrounding towns to see what arrangements we were making and went home with the intention of joining the company and meeting us in Olathe next Monday. The officers report great enthusiasm and expect to raise the whole company in this county.

Saturday, October 24, 1868

None of us worked today and all went over to town. This afternoon people came in from the country until it looked like circus day. Stoddard and Charley Finch are the center of attraction, and they are working hard to get volunteers. All of us put in a word when we can help. We ask all the boys to go with us, and most of them would go if they could.

Enough wagons and carriages have been offered to take a regiment to the railroad station. Several have said they are going who have not signed the roll. They want to know who are likely to be candidates for captain. Frank, Bill and I are strongly in favor of Charley Finch and will do all we can to have him elected. We have asked several who know him best and they tell us he is surely a wise selection and every one seems to be his friend and say they are sorry he is going to leave. We have roomed together for some time and he has treated me like a younger brother. Mr. Mitchell, for whom he has worked for several years, says a better selection could not be made.

Sunday, October 25, 1868

I go over to Wm. Corbett's today as it is my last day in Springhill for some time. I have known them nearly all my life in Indiana and they are giving me a dinner. I'll leave my trunk and belongings with them until my return. Their family consists of Mr. and Mrs. Wm. Corbett, a son, John, and two daughters, Emma and Josephine. They have a fine two-story home. John will take a load of us up to Olathe, in the morning, so I have bid the Mitchells goodbye and stay all night with John and will be one of his passengers. Frank and Bill stay all night with John Haigler at Jackson's as Haigler and Estes live there and both have enlisted. Mr. Jackson owns a grocery in town but lives on his farm adjoining on the west. Some parents must be feeling sad today, whose sons are leaving home, perhaps for the first time.

Stoddard and Finch went to Olathe today and found that Roberts had three more names on his list than they had. They have so many promised that they expect to soon pass Roberts who seems to be rather "stuck up" and that don't go with the boys. After we all get together tomorrow we will have our chance to tell what we know about Charley Finch although Stoddard's idea is that he will be captain, Roberts first and Finch second lieutenant, but the boys may change all that. We will get as many to sign the roll tomorrow as we can for only those whose names are down will get free tickets and the rest will have to pay their fare.

No one whose name is not on the roll will have a vote in selecting the officers. Stoddard and Finch have both made a promise that they would recommend me for company clerk. This office will relieve me from guard duty or any other night work. I have a diary and will keep a record of everything I know or hear while I am gone.

Monday, October 26, 1868

We leave Springhill between 7 and 8 o'clock and nearly the whole town is out to bid us goodbye. When we get to Olathe the streets down town are full of people. A vacant half block has been roped off and we who have enlisted go inside. Then those who are expecting to go are asked to go inside also. Then they are told only those who sign the roll will be given tickets and only those who have enlisted can vote for officers. The men will have several days to get acquainted and select commissioned officers. While the roll was being signed a wagon drove up with a big can of hot coffee and boxes of sandwiches and doughnuts with Charley Finch and two waiters handing them out to the boys.

Stoddard and Roberts were not in sight but we gave three hearty cheers for Charley Finch—some of us said "Captain Finch." There were several squads of ten or more headed by Ike S. Elder, Charles Streight and Andrew J. Maiden who have known Charley Finch a long time and they have posted the men in their squads. There seems to be a full company and while no one says much about it Finch seems to be a favorite. We leave Olathe a little after noon for DeSoto, the nearest railroad station on the Kansas Pacific.

Stoddard and Finch want me to take their horses overland to Topeka, and after we get about four miles out, we come to the highway from Kansas City to Lawrence and here I leave the boys and go alone toward Topeka, riding Charley's horse and leading Stoddard's. The road is fine with a nice breeze in my face, so I have a very pleasant trip ahead of me. I stop for the night—twelve miles east of Lawrence with a Scotch family who have a nice farmhouse. This is said to be the best portion of the State. There are large walnut trees along the Kaw River. The road sometimes is near the bottom lands where I can see the rich farms and heavy timber. The Scotchman and his good wife are very interesting and tell me of their home in Scotland and much about Kansas, since they live here.

Tuesday, October 27, 1868

After so much excitement yesterday I did not get to sleep very soon after retiring. The Scotch people were astir early so I got up about sunrise. After a nice breakfast I cared for my horses and started for Topeka. About 10 o'clock I crossed the road that led to Lawrence from the south. The city or town is north and across a wooden bridge, over the river, leading to it. On the south side of the road I am travelling and near where the roads cross is a large windmill on the top of a high hill. It is said to be the first grist mill in Kansas. I think it is still in operation for the great fans are going around.

I had no mishaps on the way and feed the horses and eat lunch at a roadhouse about noon. I arrived at camp near Topeka about sundown and after looking the camp all over, I found our boys at the north end near the river. It looks as if there was a full regiment here now. I passed ten companies and ours the eleventh. The boys were glad to see me, and Frank and Bill took me to their tent and introduced me to the other two in their mess.

They said they had saved a place for me and I was to share the tent with them. We had a pretty good supper and I was hungry enough to appreciate it, especially the coffee which was delicious. If we can have as good fare as this on our whole trip it will be a pleasure to go. Stoddard and Finch have taken their horses. I tried to ride Stoddard's horse part of the way but he was a "jolter" so I led him nearly all the way. After telling our experiences coming up we retired about 10 o'clock.

Wednesday, October 28, 1868

Today begins a new era in my life.   About 10 o'clock
we are called into line for the purpose of choosing company officers.   There are three candidates for the office of
captain: Henry E. Stoddard, John Roberts and Charles H.
Finch.   As the names were called those in favor of the can-
didate stepped three paces forward.   I had informed Stoddard before leaving home that all the boys in the south part
of the county wanted Charlie Finch for captain and he said
he had expected it and he would be satisfied if he got
second place.

When his name was called only six stepped forward.
Then Roberts' name was called and thirty-seven stepped
forward.   Then Finch's name was called and nearly the
whole line stepped out and all followed quickly and we
cheered.   Then Stoddard brought Finch forward and presented him to the boys as their captain.   The vote for first
lieutenant was more equal, but Stoddard received a ma-
jority of seven votes for first lieutenant.   Now there was
much dissatisfaction among Roberts' friends and he would
not accept the office of second lieutenant.   Finally he and
over twenty of his friends went over to the city and that
was the last we saw of them.   There were between twenty
and thirty came in from Paola who had been enrolled by
W. S. Tilton and these were added to our company, making
it complete and Tilton was elected second lieutenant.

Thursday, October 29, 1868

Our camp is about a mile below the city and quite near
the river.   We have to use the river water for cooking our
meals, also to drink.   We eat only two meals a day and
each man has been given a blanket on his arrival so we
are "roughing it" until we can draw our regular equipment.   A camp guard has been placed around the camp

except along the river. If it were not so, none of the farmers would have any poultry in a few days. No one can go over to town without a pass from the adjutant. Some go to the river for water and then slip by the guard and go over to town. After noon we are called into line again and a man made a little speech telling us what was expected of us as soldiers, after which we were sworn into the service of the U. S. as L Troop of the 19th Kansas Volunteer Cavalry.

We have been kept pretty busy and some of the boys have had to do guard duty around the camp. Others spend their time devising a way to slip by the guard into a brush thicket near the river, for if they get into the brush they will be hidden from the camp and can go to the city unchallenged. A detail of four men from each company have to do guard duty daily and some of them never look back while pacing their beat so their friends can slip out unseen.

Friday, October 30, 1868

I am getting acquainted with several of the boys. There is a "chuck-a-luck" game operating inside the camp guard and the operator is getting a good share of the boys' spare change. We drew "A" tents today and have set them up. There are five in our tent. My partners are W. F. Doty, W. J. Radenbocker, Oscar O. Lee and Alfred W. Wood. We get a pass to go outside the guard to get an armful of hay for our bed so we will sleep more comfortably. The ground is a little too hard, but the hay makes a pretty good substitute for spring mattresses.

Frank and Bill are pretty good story tellers and give us their experience with people in Missouri where they came from. It is the way they tell their stories which makes them interesting. Lee has red hair and is very freckled and his laugh is comical. Wood is rather quiet but his conversation indicates that he had a pretty good education and knows more than he cares to tell. One of our men got outside today and was not in his mess tonight. He was one of Roberts' recruits and it is thought by his partners that he has deserted.

Saturday, October 31, 1868

The nights and mornings are quite cool now. We go to bed early as our allowance of wood is small and it is too cold to be without fire, so we go to bed early and talk, sing or tell stories, until some neighbor yells "Shut up."

We get up when we get ready unless our cook calls "Breakfast," then all hurry for our bacon, crackers and coffee. We draw ourselves Army clothing this morning and I am detailed company clerk and have to go to work at our company headquarters, but sleep in my own tent with the boys.

Capt. Finch has informed me that I am to keep a record of everything the company received and charge the boys with whatever is issued to them in the way of equipment, including their clothing. I find it a considerable job, but I am to be free from all other duties except I will have to care for my horse. I will have a good chance to see the real life of a soldier and not experience all its hardships. Lieut. Tilton is assisting me to get the books started.

Sunday, November 1, 1868

This is our first Sunday in camp and a beautiful day. Many came over from the city, some on foot and many in carriages. There was preaching in camp this afternoon and after the services a lot of Bibles and Testaments were distributed to the boys. I had to work in our office and did not get to attend the services or get a book. Our visitors all expressed a desire that we would have a good time and return safely. Many would shake hands with the boys, a good many of whom were young ladies. The boys were on their good behavior and willing to shake hands with all the young ladies and their mammas.

Tonight it is very different. Some donned their citizen clothes and went out with the visitors and now there is whisky in camp, and the noise is the effect of it. Several are now in the guard house, others ought to be.

Monday, November 2, 1868

We draw our saddles and saddle blankets, bridles, spurs and lariats this forenoon and this afternoon we draw our horses. One hundred horses are tied to a heavy rope stretched to two large posts and as each man's name is called he steps out and unties a horse and leads him away. No one has a choice of horses as they are taken in rotation.

When my turn came I led my horse out and jumped on him bareback but forgot that I had put my spurs on so was soon going on the run. I was sticking the spurs in him to hold on. I finally got him headed for the next company line. When he hit the line or rope he stopped. I went on and came down between two horses on the other side unhurt. I then led him back to our company and Sergt. Streight wanted to trade with me and when I refused he finally gave me $10 and the one I now have is quiet and gentle. I work the rest of the day and tonight on the muster rolls which gives a description of each man. I do not get through until late and when I get to my tent the boys are all asleep. Have only been to town once to get a tin cup and wash pan.

Tuesday, November 3, 1868

Get up earlier than usual and take a walk around the camp. Can see the new State House which is much higher than any of the others. It is not yet finished but seems to be a very large and costly edifice. After breakfast I went to work on the muster rolls which I finished by noon. Capt. Finch got me a pass to the city this afternoon to see the sights. The new State House is a very imposing building, covering a whole block, but is only partly completed. It is located near the main part of the city and on a main street just west of the principal avenue. I met Frank Doty on the street, when we take tramps in different directions and find the city is not very large as we soon came to where the houses were few and far between. The city is longest north and south, and does not extend over two miles from the river in that direction.

I met a boy from Company K named Orlando Soward whom I knew in Indiana twelve years ago when his parents moved to Kansas and now live near Junction City. This is election day and the boys can only vote for President. When I get back to camp they want me to vote, but I will not be 21 until next February. They insist I must be 21 or I could not enlist so I finally go and cast my first vote for U. S. Grant. No one challenged my vote as no one except our officers knew my age.

Wednesday, November 4, 1868

We draw our guns and twenty rounds of ammunition this afternoon. Our guns are the Spencer carbine, thirty inches long with a cartridge magazine holding seven cartridges. These are thrown into the barrel by a lever which is also a guard over the small trigger underneath. They are carried on horseback by a strap over the shoulder that holds them diagonally across our backs, making them easy to carry and not in the way while riding. No sabres or revolvers were issued. I go to town again today and send my citizens' clothing by express to Corbett's at Springhill. When I return I find there is considerable excitement in camp. They have orders to be ready to march by daylight tomorrow.

This camp has been named Camp Crawford in honor of the Governor of the State. I also learned that Governor Crawford has resigned and will command our regiment. He has the reputation for being a very fine gentleman, kind to all who have met him in any way. The other officers as far as I have learned are Lieut.-Col., Horace L. Moore; Majors, Wm. C. Jones, Richard C. Jenkins and Charles Dimon; Adjt., J. M. Steele; Surgeon, Marion Bailey; Quartermaster, Luther A. Thresher; Commissary, John Johnston; Chief Bugler, Wm. Gruber.

Thursday, November 5, 1868

We are up early and have our horses fed and groomed ready to go, but the orders now are to be ready to march at 10 o'clock, so we stand around and talk and joke. We have not forgotten to prepare a lunch to eat on the way as it is not likely we will stop until we camp tonight. Finally the bugle sounds to advance and all are in the saddle and on our way towards the city. When we come to Grand Avenue, we are met by the band and march south. The streets are lined with people on both sides for several blocks, shouting, "Goodbye, boys, and good luck to you." All the boys rode bareheaded and many of them smiled at the girls who waved their handkerchiefs. It was certainly an earnest farewell which all of us greatly appreciated. Our destination is Post Wichita on the Arkansas River, 160 miles from Topeka. In about an hour we lose sight of the capitol building, the last one seen.

We camp for the night on Wakarusha Creek, twelve miles from Topeka. A load of hay has been furnished each company, also a load of provisions. Each horse has one quart of corn, and rations issued to ten messes to each company which they are to divide fairly. We left our "A" tents in Camp Crawford and have one-half a dog tent to the man which can be buttoned together and makes a small tent or cover for a bed. The weather is so pleasant that we just put part of the tent on the ground and the beds and the rest on top. We sit around our campfire until after 9 o'clock talking of our trip, where we are going and what we will do when we get there.

Friday, November 6, 1868

We have reveille at 4 o'clock when every man has to get up and fall in line for rollcall. Orderly Sergt. Ike S. Elder then calls the company roll and every man answers to his name as it is called. Then comes stable call, when we feed and groom our horses. Then comes breakfast, after which our bedding and cooking utensils are loaded into the company wagon and we are ready to go. We march at 6, and pass through Burlingame about 11 o'clock.

We noticed a good many black-looking rocks which have the appearance of coal. We have marched about twenty-five miles today and I have been at the front of the company, sometimes with Lieut. Tilton who is about my age—he is not yet 21. He came from Iowa a year ago to Paola where he taught school last winter. He served for a time in an Iowa regiment at the close of the Civil War. We have worked together for the last ten days but have been so busy on the books that we did not get acquainted. I think we are likely to be very good friends later.

I also get better acquainted with Orderly Sergt. Ike S. Elder, Sergts. Streight and Maiden. Col. Crawford did not leave Topeka with us, but is expected to follow and join us later. We camp for the night on Elm Creek where we had plenty of wood and water. The horses are taken to a place below the camp to water them.

Saturday, November 7, 1868

The excitement having worn out, we slept much better last night, but go the same routine—rise at 4, breakfast and march at 6. The country passed through was similar to that of yesterday except there were no black rocks. There is very little timber except along the creeks where a few oak trees are scattered around, but there is more or less underbrush. It has been cloudy all day and after crossing the Neosho River we camp near the river on our right or west side. The river makes a big bend here and runs to the south or nearly so. We march about twenty-five miles today and are two miles from the town of Emporia.

Col. Crawford has arrived. He is now ex-Governor, having resigned to take charge of our regiment. He had only a few months more to serve, as his successor has been elected, but the Lieutenant-Governor will finish his term. Our mess is the same as it was at Camp Crawford. We have found a way to get across the river. By wading to a small island through shallow water to the other side is a large fallen tree, so we can cross the deep main channel on the fallen tree. After dark Doty, "Raden" and I cross the river and soon find a farm house and finally find a tree (fruit tree) loaded with (feathered) fruit and we pick one each and go back the way we came. On the island we build a fire and have a lunch of roast chicken. Because I cleaned and roasted a gizzard the boys call me "Gizzard," but we had a good time and perhaps the last chicken we will have for many months.

Sunday, November 8, 1868

It began to rain in the night but we had set up our dog tents and spread our rubber blankets on the ground so we did not get wet. We did not get started until nearly 8 o'clock. We passed through Emporia about an hour later. The rain had ceased and all the people were out to see us pass. This was the last town we have seen and it has a small population, perhaps 250, and the buildings are all wooden, no sidewalks and the streets are not even graded. After leaving the town we pass very few houses all the rest of the day. We have been going up Cottonwood Creek and camp near the creek. There are a good many trees and brush but the stream is only a few feet wide.

We put up our tents because it is very cloudy and looks like rain. While eating supper it began to rain. There are no houses or signs of any one living near. I hear the Cottonwood Falls above our camp but there can not be much of a waterfall from what we see in the creek. It began to rain so hard that we had to crawl into our tent to keep dry. Some of the boys have built a big fire and are out in the rain around the fire singing and making a big noise. We hear the water in the creek so it must be rising and we are on pretty low ground.

Monday, November 9, 1868

It rained very hard during the night and the water came in our tent and woke us by coming through our blankets. We crawl out in the rain, hunt our clothes, pull out our bed, pull down our tent, and wade to higher ground. By the time we had secured all our property the water was several inches deep and we were wet through and cold. With chattering teeth we at last found some dry wood and revived the fire which had not been entirely put out by the rain. It stopped raining an hour or so before daylight and we had our bedding on picket ropes stretched around the fire. The captain and lieutenants have "A" tents.

Finch and Stoddard have occupied one and Lieut. Tilton and Sergt. Elder the other. This morning Finch and Stoddard have a little scrap and Stoddard is in the cook tent, Finch in the "A" tent, so they have to make a change as they had to have a cook tent for all. Finally Stoddard has Tilton to change places with him. Now each tent wants a cook. Capt. Finch asked me to come and cook for his mess. We have taken a day to decide. Stoddard wants Haigler to take care of his horse besides cooking while Finch says he will care for his own horse.

It snowed today for the first time this winter. Haigler and I ride together today and talk over the cooking proposition and agree to try it. So tonight I told Charley I was no cook but thought I could boil water and fry bacon so I am to make a trial. We had a pretty good supper and they said I would do. Haigler and I move our beds to the cook tent. As we are both from Springhill we get along all right. We have only army rations now.

Tuesday, November 10, 1868

We are up at 4 and have fried potatoes and bacon. I got some pointers from Haigler and cooked a pot of beans last night for today. I am no cook, in my own estimation, but they think I am doing pretty well and will soon learn to be a "regular" chef.

We passed a man this morning who was at work building a cabin. Said he was starting a town and was naming it Eldorado. After we marched twenty-five miles we camp near a small creek with plenty of trees. There is a settler cabin near our camp and some of the officers are having the woman bake biscuits for their supper. Haigler and I go to see if we can get some but there are a lot ahead of us. I went back to our tent while Haigler waited our turn. After supper I went to relieve him. Pretty soon the husband came out and told us the flour was nearly gone, and if some one would keep his wife in fire wood he would go to a neighbor's and get some more. I volunteered and had several armloads in the house and still he did not come. She told me to sit down by the fire until he came back.

The woman asked me where I came from and when I said "Indiana" she told me she was also a Hoosier. I asked her how she came to be here. She said: "During the Civil War we girls knit socks for the soldiers and I put my name and address in a pair I knit and my husband got it and wrote me. He was in an Illinois regiment so when he returned home he came to see me and a year later we were married. He bought this claim of a soldier whose intended would not come out here, so he had to give up his claim or lose his sweetheart. We have been here only a few months."

The husband came about 9 with a sack of flour but had to go eight miles for it. They gave me my supper of bacon and biscuit and enough biscuit for our breakfast. This is the only house we have seen today so we are about beyond all civilization. When I got back to our tent Haigler was asleep but we had biscuit for breakfast.

Wednesday, November 11, 1868

We are awakened every morning by the bugle call at 4 o'clock, but we do not get in line to march before 6. We have not seen a house or settler all day, neither have we seen an Indian. The scouts say there are no Indians within a hundred miles. Our provisions are pretty low, but we expect more at Post Wichita. The day is delightful and the boys are in a jolly mood, singing songs and cheering, once in a while.

The full regiment did not come with us. Company M
went to Fort Hays to guard a provision train and meet us
somewhere on the Canadian River. They were to go on the
railroad from Topeka to Fort Hays. We must be near
Wichita. Gen. Sheridan is somewhere on the North Canadian with Gen. Custer and his 7th Cavalry and we are to
meet them at their headquarters. As soon as we join them
we are to proceed against the hostile Indians supposed to
be only a few miles from where the cavalry are now located.

We only march eighteen miles today and have a good
camping place on a small stream with plenty of oak timber
along both banks. Near the stream is sycamore and hackberry trees. We hear the boys complain because they
have nothing for supper, for rations have given out.

Thursday, November 12, 1868

We made twenty miles by 3 P. M. and when the boys
came in sight of the post they cheered heartily. We camp
on the east side of the river a few hundred yards below the
post building. There is only one building, a long adobe with
a wood "lean-to." There are only a sergeant and ten men
here. We draw five days' rations from what they have and
the boys are happy since they have all they want to eat.
Stoddard and Finch are all right again and Haigler will do
their cooking and I am relieved. I was going to quit my job
anyway.

The river bottom is covered with many large fallen cottonwood trees, which have been cut down to furnish feed
for horses when the ground is covered with snow, for they
eat the twigs and bark instead of hay. There is very little
water in the river. The Little Arkansas empties into the
main river a mile above the post. The river bottom is several miles wide and the channel is about a mile wide, when

the water is high; but now there is only sand to be seen besides the trees that have been cut and have fallen in all directions.

Friday, November 13, 1868

We do not march today. We have drawn soap, and the boys are cleaning up and washing their clothes. We had inspection this afternoon. We are called out in line and the officers examine our horses, equipment, guns and clothing. One man was told to wash his hands and face cleaner.

This has been an outpost for several years to supply the nearest forts when necessary. The men tell us we will see plenty of buffaloes within twenty miles of here. We will then have plenty of fresh meat instead of Army bacon. Some of the boys went hunting among the trees and logs near the water, but there was only one rabbit brought in.

Saturday November 14, 1868

We are in the saddle at 6, and across the river by 7 where we pass an old corral or pen where stock had been kept. Our destination now is Camp Supply on the North Canadian River at the mouth of Beaver Creek. We have 198 miles to go and if we eat as heartily every day we will have to live on buffalo most of the time, unless a train with provisions meets us before we get there. It is expected we can get through all right, as we will be in the buffalo range and can have fresh meat every day. We cannot expect to make the trip under a week and will have to make roads for the wagon train.

We have several scouts to guide us to our destination— Apache Bill, Johnny Stillwell and Captain Pliley of Company A. None of them were ever over this route before. Pliley and Stillwell were scouts for Col. Forsyth last year and were in the fight at Beecher's Island on the Arickaree

JACK STILLWELL, A NOTED SCOUT WITH THE
19TH KANSAS VOLUNTEERS

—From the Collection of E. A. Brininstool.

in Colorado. They crawled through the Indian lines and brought relief to the besieged soldiers.

We have no roads to follow and the scouts and advance guard have to find one. We have a pioneer corps to make the roads across ravines and creeks, also a rear guard to pick up stragglers or anything lost from the wagons. We saw large herds of buffaloes this afternoon and hunters were sent out to bring in fresh meat for the regiment. Sergt. Streight has gone from our company.

We have only gone fifteen miles today but had to make roads for the wagons and we stopped to graze our horses a couple of times. The grass is very good in this valley. The hunters killed several buffaloes and I ate buffalo meat for the first time. It is much better than Army bacon, but we had to fry some bacon for grease to fry our buffalo meat. We have very little salt or pepper and fresh meat takes lots of it. I have been riding with Sergt. Maiden today. He and Streight are in the same mess. They are both fine fellows.

Sunday, November 15, 1868

Our camp is up at the usual hour but we do not get started until nearly 7. In a couple of hours we see very large herds of buffaloes. The plains look black for miles, they are so close together. The same hunters go out again today and were soon among them shooting when some one yelled "Here comes the buffaloes!" Sure enough they were coming toward us. We had orders to halt, and our company was in the front. The buffaloes passed within fifty feet of us for nearly half an hour. Every man in the regiment fired on them but very few were hit. In the excitement the men forgot to use the rear sight on their guns, so shot too high. A few of the herd were a little distance to one side and when they came to our line we had to open ranks and let them go through. One man's horse became very much excited so did not get out of the way when a buffalo ran into him, throwing horse and rider to the ground. Neither was seriously hurt. After all had passed there were several buffaloes so seriously wounded they fell out of the herd. Hunters went out and killed them, but some showed fight. Our company had a whole buffalo and part of several more, so everybody had all the fresh meat they wanted for supper and breakfast and only the choicest steaks were cooked and eaten.

It has been cold and rainy since 3 o'clock and while we are not wet, our boots are soaked, so one's feet get cold. We camped tonight on Nescatunga Creek in a grove of trees which are a protection to our horses. The camp is in a very sandy place and the sand is piled up in places, so only the tops of the greasewood brush can be seen. Frank, Bill and I dig into a sand hill and make a bed, covering it with our rubber blankets. We then go out and pull a lot of grass for our horses and cover them with our saddle blankets. By this time the wind is blowing a blizzard from the north and freezing cold. We build a big company fire, but cannot get warm. We go to bed and nearly freeze although the wind does not blow on us.

We have not experienced such cold weather before and many of the boys say if they were home they would stay there. I felt the same way during the night, for it was almost impossible to sleep on account of the severe cold. Had the horses not been blanketed well, and sheltered by the trees, some would have frozen to death. It was so cold that the camp guard was called in, or they would have frozen to death.

Monday, November 16, 1868

The wind blew a hurricane in the night and the air was freezing cold this morning. My boots were frozen, although covered with blankets beside my bed. The creek froze over during the night and we had to break the ice an inch thick to water our horses.

The wind blew down nearly every "A" tent in the regiment. The ground was so sandy the stakes did not hold. Stoddard's tent was blown about twenty feet when they tied a rope around a tree and crawled under it. Some had been tied to trees by one or more ropes so did not get away. The camp looked like a wreck this morning. It was getting daylight when we crawled out. Capt. Finch and Lieut. Tilton crawled out from under their tent which was flat. We got started at 7 and had to break the ice across the creek so as to go up on the north side.

It got warmer by night and we camped on a creek with very little wood or water. Our horses get a quart of corn and graze as long as we can see. We march only nineteen miles and going is slow.

Tuesday, November 17, 1868

It was not so cold last night, although there was frost this morning, and the day has moderated considerable. We have now passed beyond the timber and no trees can be seen, even along the creeks. We camp about 3 o'clock and as we have no hay we take our horses out to graze. There is more grass here than we have seen lately and we have one man in every "four" take four horses, tie their lariats together and hold them to graze in the best place to be found.

As there is no wood the rest of the boys take saddle blankets and hunt dry "buffalo chips" with which they get supper, for they make a hot fire if dry enough. There had been a good many buffaloes here several months previously. We have lots of fun over our fuel, and no one would think how near we came to freezing last night.

I go up to see the officers of the company once in a while and see how Haigler gets along. No one has gone after the deserters, and no one seems to care or blame them, for we are having a pretty tough trip some days and our fare is not as it was, for our salt is gone.

Wednesday, November 18, 1868

We got a pretty early start this morning and the country is comparatively level. We make thirty-two miles. We have a roadometer on the ambulance we have with our train. We did not have to stop to wait for the wagons as there were no very bad crossings. Our hunters keep us supplied with meat and we are now wishing we had some of the "good old bacon" again. Our camp tonight is on Medicine Lodge Creek with very few small cottonwoods, but considerable drift wood to cook with.

About sundown while the horses were still out grazing, a man saw a piece of wood that he wanted to secure, so he tied his lariat to his saddle that he had taken off, and went to secure the piece of wood. His horse soon had gone far enough to tighten the rope and when the saddle came toward him he took fright and ran toward the herd, with the saddle flying after him. This frightened the herd, so the boys could not hold them, some got away and some of the men were dragged some distance before they would let them go. One man got fast in the lariats and was dragged a mile and was nearly dead when found. His name is Robert McCleary of Company L.

I had just tied my horse to a wagon, but had been out and gathered or pulled a blanket full of grass while my horse was grazing so he would have a feed in the morning. Men are out in all directions hunting horses tonight.

Thursday, November 19, 1868

We did not march today and many are out looking for horses. Capts. Finch and Pliley have taken two days rations and gone back to overtake horses that have taken the back track. Lieut. Tilton and I go out on foot toward the west to see what we can see to shoot, so I take my gun along. We saw something about a quarter of a mile away, but could not tell whether it was an antelope or coyote. I shot at it a couple of times, but it soon was over the hill. I then killed a prairie dog to see what it looked like. Our rations are all gone so none are issued except as we kill it. I have saved up five or six hardtack.

It will be buffalo meat or nothing from now on until we get to Camp Supply, or a train meets us. After the day's hunt for horses there are ten men in our company who will have to walk or ride in the wagons. Poor Bob McCleary seems to be hurt seriously.

Friday, November 20, 1868

We are in our saddles again by 7 o'clock. Ten men in our company and nearly 100 in the regiment have no horses. These men are put in the rear of the column and in front of the wagons. At the first stop some of them come to their companies and the boys give them a ride for a few miles while they walk beside their horses.

We march twenty-five miles today and camp on a creek where there is plenty of good wood and water. Capts. Finch and Pliley came in tonight but had no horses. They said there were several going back, but were on the home

run and had too much start. They said they must have
followed them fifty miles and did not even see one of them.

Our wagons did not get in tonight until about 9 o'clock.
We have plenty of meat but no salt, nor bread, which is
rather unsavory food. Hardtack is a legal tender now.
I bought a Testament of Cyrus Campbell for six hardtack.
I only had eight. He got the book at Topeka one Sunday when they were given to the boys. We have nothing
to read at all, and so I had good reading.

We are expecting to meet a supply train in this part of
the country. The scouts are out trying to locate it. We
see smoke in the west and think it must be the train to
meet us.

Saturday, November 21, 1868

With hopeful expectations we start at 6:30 expecting to
have a feast before night. We are nearly beyond the buffalo ranges and they are very scarce. Only a few "rene-
gades"—those driven out of the herds—are seen now and
when killed are usually miles away and are not brought
into camp until late. After marching sixteen miles we arrive at the creek where the train was expected to be found.
No train had come to meet us although the scouts had
gone ten miles or more up and down the creek but no sign
of wagons or trail. We have plenty of wood and water,
also good grazing for our horses, but all of us are very
much disappointed and considerable grumbling is heard
but we have not lost hope.

The officers' stores are all gone, so they are in the same
condition as the men. Coffee and some sugar is all there
is in the commissary now. I got some salt from a teamster
and our only food now is "jerked" buffalo—thin slices

roasted over coals until well done. Some of the teamsters who have been on the plains for years have taught us how to prepare buffalo meat so it will keep a long time and tastes very good without bread, but it is not very good unless salted. We have meat tonight, but it was an "old timer" and very tough, but we "jerked" him just the same as if he had been younger.

Sunday, November 22, 1868

We got up this morning covered with snow several inches deep. We did not put up our tent because it was almost clear. It is still snowing when we get up. Capt. Pliley with sixty men has been detailed to go in search of food for we must be within a few days' march of Camp Supply.

We and others have the same idea that our destination, Camp Supply, cannot be more than fifty miles distant. We take up our line of march through snow several inches deep, leading our horses most of the time for now the grass is covered and they, like ourselves, are without food. Some of the men have frozen feet and have to ride if they have horses, and in the wagons if not.

Our orders today are, no man is to ride his horse without permission, so we walk. The only food the horses can get is from green cottonwood trees if we find any to cut down. The snow has been falling all day, hard at times, and buffaloes could not be seen at any distance so the hunters could not go very far from the command, fearing they might get lost. We only get one small ration, which was only a few bites per man. We camp in heavy timber with plenty of wood and water and have a big company fire and sleep in the snow.

Monday, November 23, 1868

It is still snowing this morning and we do not march to-day. It is not cold in the timber with a big fire as there is plenty of dry wood from fallen trees.

Our hunters are out today but the snow is so blinding and the wind so cold that they return in a few hours with no success. We have no food so we just spread our ponchos on the snow and make our beds on them a little distance from the fire. We have a great pile of dry wood and we sit or stand around the fire and listen to the boys tell what they will do when they get to Camp Supply. When some one begins to curse the Government or some one for our condition, everyone jumps on him, calls him a growler or tells him he will know how to appreciate a "square meal" when we get to camp. The idea is to be cheerful under any circumstances and if we don't feel that way it is wise to keep still.

Tuesday, November 24, 1868

We march this morning through snow about twenty inches deep, we know not where, but keep on, leading our horses. We have no roads to follow. Sometimes we are on the top of a ridge but soon down in a ravine. About 9 A. M. a buffalo was killed, when we stopped and got a few bites to the man or 1-1000th part of a buffalo.

Some of the advance guard saw him and killed him. After a little over an hour halt we again started on, and by evening we camped in a grove of hackberry trees with berries still on them. There were only four men of our company to form the line for camp. I was one of the four. All the others had fallen out and were marching more slowly. We were ready to stop and it was an hour or more before all were in. The wagons had to go into Camp 4, miles back, because they could not cross a ravine. We are all having hackberries for our supper. We eat them seeds and all and they taste pretty good. We can eat almost anything just now.

Lieut. Stoddard had put his coffee pot and some coffee in the company wagon and asked me to go back to the wagons to get them. I tried to get out of going, by saying I was too tired and would not ride my horse so he told me to take his horse, and when I saw he was fully determined to have his coffee I told him if he wanted it that bad to go after it himself. He then ordered me to go and I refused, so he called a corporal and guards to place me under arrest, for disobedience. When they got there and he told them to arrest me, I got my gun and told them to keep back. While we were in that position Capt. Finch came in from a hunt and wanted to know the particulars.

Stoddard told him that I had refused to obey orders and he was placing me under arrest. After he heard Stoddard's story he asked me why I had disobeyed. I told him that I had not been on my horse all day and was completely tired out, while he had ridden nearly all the time, and it was he that wanted the coffee, so I told him to go get it. Then they talked awhile until Stoddard got excited and called Finch a "liar" and got choked for it. In the meantime I was getting out of sight, and did not wait to see how they settled it. They did not call me back and I heard no more about it.

Wednesday, November 25, 1868

The wagons got in about 9 this forenoon and all they contained to eat was forty pounds of cube sugar in officers' stores. This was issued to the regiment and there were only three cubes to the man. Some of the boys were up in hackberry trees and would not come down for sugar, so did not get any. Some of the trees were full of berries which most of the boys said were delicious and ate all they wanted.

The companies are called in line this afternoon and the best mounts are selected to go on. Those whose horses are too weak to travel are to stay here, while the others are to go to camp and get relief to them.

Capt. Payne is to pilot about 700 of the regiment to Camp Supply and if we do not meet Pliley with relief, will try and find it somewhere. We get started about 3 P. M. and soon cross a large stream. The water was so clear I emptied my canteen and filled it with fresh water. A little later I thought I would take a drink from my canteen and to my surprise it was so salty I could not possibly drink it.

We marched until after 10 o'clock, leading our horses most of the time. We have nothing to eat and go to bed as soon as we can find a good place to lie down. It has been decided to send hunters on both flanks and if there is any game to bring it in at once.

Thursday, November 26, 1868

If we were back in civilization today it would very likely be Thanksgiving Day. We think we are having a pretty hard time, but when we look at it as a day of thanksgiving we realize that we still have many things to be thankful for. We are all in good health and many back home are not. We have had no serious accidents or deaths in the regiment.

The snow is melting, making it very disagreeable walking. Our horses have very poor grazing and we stop when we come to a patch of tall grass that appears to be good feed, and graze our horses. Some of the horses are getting pretty weak and we have to go slow and stop often until the snow is gone and the feed is uncovered.

We went into camp about sundown in a canyon where there is a dry bed of a river, except a tiny stream. We are fortunate tonight to have a buffalo. I make good use of the salty water I saved in my canteen. We cut the meat in small strips, put it in the salt water a few minutes and then hold it over the coals with a long stick. We eat it before it gets fully "jerked" but it certainly is fine eating with seasoning.

Friday, November 27, 1868

We are up at 4 and finish our buffalo meat for breakfast. We have no wagons with us, and go as far as our horses can stand. We ride and walk by turns. We stop occasionally to graze the horses. We must have travelled thirty miles today. We walked so much in the wet snow that our boots leak and our feet are wet all the time, which is very disagreeable. We have a small buffalo today for 700 men, so we do not have a feast.

Our camp is on the Canadian River, but do not find Camp Supply. The scouts have gone up and down the river on both sides and have found no wagon trails, so conclude we are too far down the river, or we would find a wagon road. We had expected to find the camp near where we came to the river, so we are again disappointed and will have to go hungry a while longer.

Saturday, November 28, 1868

It has been decided that we go up the river without crossing. We get started at daylight and we expect to surely find the camp today. We make good time and if there is a camp on this river we are sure to find it pretty soon.

Our company is in the rear today and after noon we heard those ahead cheering heartily, and we began to cheer too, not knowing what it was all about, but pretty soon a trooper came hurrying back and informed us that Camp

Supply was only five miles ahead. Then we *did* cheer, and kept it up for a long time. We arrived at Camp Supply early in the afternoon and drew rations.

Some of us ate too much bacon raw. We also drew feed for our horses and after they had a good feed, the cook said "Eat" and we ate too much, and some were awfully sick.

I certainly enjoyed that meal and the coffee was the best I ever drank. The commissary said he never saw such a hungry lot of fellows. Our rations did not last long, but no more tonight.

Sunday, November 29, 1868

We drew rations again this morning. We also have "A" tents, for our dog tents were so worn and torn that they were almost useless. Captain Pliley had been here several days and as the best wagons had gone north, they set blacksmiths, harnessmakers and wagonmakers to work to repair the wagons and harness left behind, so with the mules left for use around the post he had a small train of twelve wagons ready to start with provisions to relieve the boys left behind, near Salt Creek in the hackberry grove. Maj. Dimon went in charge of the train and Capt. Pliley as scout. Several of our officers also went along to see if they were still there, for they had nothing to eat when we left them, except hackberries.

A portion of M Troop of our regiment went as guard to the train. None of us who had been there volunteered to return. We expect to stay here until our horses recruit, so they can make a trip into the Indian country. The weather since our arrival has been delightful.

This is to be a supply post for the Army operating in this part of the country. Several new buildings are going up, one quite large, to be used as a storehouse for supplies for the Army. Gen. Sheridan and some infantry are stationed here, but Gen. Custer and the 7th Cavalry have gone on an expedition into the Indian country. He waited for our arrival until the 23rd, when his command started out in a big snowstorm with the band playing at the head of the column.

Col. Crawford reported to Gen. Sheridan this morning. Our camp is about a mile from the post and near Beaver Creek, where there is pretty good pasture for our horses. Nothing has been heard from Custer's command since they left over a week ago and Gen. Sheridan is very anxious for news of his whereabouts.

Monday, November 30, 1868

We draw more tents today and are quite comfortable. We have plenty of soap and water and we can hardly recognize each other since we have turned white and have good clothes.

We are now among the U. S. troops and have orders to look our best for we may have to be inspected by regular officers. We all have to do work on our camp. The tents have to be in perfect line to a rope stretched for that purpose. The company street has to be made level, so we have not had much time to take in our surroundings. A scout came in this evening and reported that Gen. Custer's command had a fight with the Indians last Friday and defeated them with great loss to the Indians and his own loss was considerable. We are anxious to hear particulars.

Tuesday, December 1, 1868

This is a beautiful day. About 8 o'clock we hear that the 7th Cavalry is about ten miles out and will arrive about noon with a lot of Indian prisoners captured in the fight of a few days ago. We have orders to be in readiness to receive them on their arrival about 11 o'clock. We march over to the post and there we are given a position where we are to await their arrival.

Shortly after noon an officer came into camp and informed Gen. Sheridan that the heroes were within a mile of the post, and we were so informed. In a short time we saw a troop of Indians approaching. These were the Osage guides and trailers, painted in colors with war paint. They were chanting their war songs and firing their guns in the air every few minutes and giving war whoops.

Next came the white scouts riding four abreast, led by their chief, California Joe, on his mule and his pipe in his mouth. Behind these came the Indian prisoners on ponies, but under guard. These prisoners had brought their best costumes of bright colors and some had bright red blankets. (They were the best dressed of all the parade.) Some distance in the rear rode the troops, formed in column of platoon.

The leading platoon, composed of sharpshooters under command of Col. Cook, and preceded by the band playing "Garry Owen" (Gen. Custer's favorite), was followed in succession by the squadrons in the regular order of march.

In this order they marched on to the parade ground and as they passed Gen. Sheridan, the officers gave a salute with the sabre, which was returned by him, by gracefully lifting his cap and smiling. We took no part in this review but were given a chance to witness it and it was the subject of our conversation for some time.

Wednesday, December 2, 1868

We are anxious to hear all about the fight and get a better view of Gen. Custer, as he was dressed like a scout yesterday and we did not recognize him, so we are hoping to get a better view of him. We are also wondering what will

CALIFORNIA JOE (MOSES MILNER).

Courtesy of the Kansas State Historical Society.

come next, where we will have a chance to mix up with the redskins.

We have some of the particulars of the fight today. The troops left here on Monday of last week and came onto a trail leading south which they followed until Thursday night when the Osage scouts reported a camp not far ahead. They waited in the snow for the plan of attack to be outlined and about 3 A. M. the four battalions were given orders to attack on four sides of the camp at once.

Maj. Elliott was sent out first and given a position in the rear of the camp; the sides were given to Col. Thompson and Maj. White. The front was led by Col. Cook at the head of the sharpshooters. The other two companies were under the command of Col. West and Capt. Hamilton.

The fight began at the earliest dawn and when the bugle sounded "Charge," the entire command dashed into the camp. The Indians were taken entirely by surprise and only had time to grab guns or bow and arrows, whichever was handy. Some did not have time to get ammunition for their guns. This accounts for the small loss of life in the ranks.

The command stayed all day near the camp, destroying everything they could find. Killed nearly 800 ponies, which was the greatest loss to the Indians. It was found during the late afternoon that Maj. Elliott and about twenty men were missing. After hunting around where the fighting had taken place, their bodies could not be found, and the searchers had to leave them behind, knowing they had been killed at some place not far away.

The body of Capt. Hamilton was brought in with the wounded, among whom was Capt. Barnitz. Black Kettle and 103 warriors were the dead Indians gathered on the battle field.

Now that we are with the Regular Army we have to do as they do. We are taught the bugle calls and have to obey them as follows: Roll call at 4 A. M.; breakfast at 6; stable call at 7; guard mount at 8; take our horses to graze from 9 to 11; dinner call at 12. From 2 to 4 we graze our horses, then at sundown retreat; tattoo at 8:45 and taps at 9, when all lights must be put out in the tents but our campfires are allowed to burn out. We can lie in bed and talk without light.

Our camp is a quarter mile from that of the 7th Cavalry and while we have met some of the soldiers we have not seen Gen. Custer. His men say he is a fine fellow, kind to them and will share with a private who is in need.

Thursday, December 3, 1868

We each had a full ration last night and I ate too much so am not feeling first rate. It rained during the night and this morning. It is cloudy and the snow is all gone but tonight it turns colder. Our camp is on the west bank of Beaver Creek and a half mile from the Canadian. There is timber and brush along the river but none along the creek, but there is plenty of tall grass and one man takes four horses to graze, while the other men have to keep the camp neat and clean, get wood and fill the nose bags and help the cook.

Friday, December 4, 1868

As company clerk, I have been exempt from guard duty, but Capt. Finch being absent, Lieut. Stoddard is in command of the company and now has an opportunity to get the best of me for my disobedience at Hackberry Camp. He has gone to the adjutant and told him that there was nothing for the company clerk to do and would like him to give him an order that I report for duty. He gave the order to the sergeant and told him it show it to me and have me at roll call next morning.

Next morning Lieut. Tilton attended roll call and I was not in line. Stoddard then went to the sergeant and told him to see that I was there next time, so I answered from my bed, but he saw I was not in line and he gave orders for me to be put on extra duty. I asked the orderly what he had for me to do and he told me there were a few post holes to dig for the posts to which our big company picket line was to be tied. That was too much punishment for I knew the boys would smile at me, if they did not say anything, so I told the sergeant I was not feeling well enough to work, but was going up to see the doctor at sick call.

When I arrived the doctor said, "Well, young man, what is the matter with you?"

I told him I thought I had been eating too much since our arrival. He told me to stick out my tongue and then told his orderly to give me some kind of medicine and I took it gladly. Then he said for me to keep quiet a couple of days and eat less and I would be all right. I asked him to give me an excuse from duty and he ordered his clerk to give it to me. Lieut. Stoddard or no one else could force me to work for two days, and I hoped Capt. Finch would return by that time.

We have to make the best of everything that comes our way, so at roll call some of the boys help the orderly sergeant get the men out of bed or they would not get up. If they resist they are pulled out of the tent and have to get in line undressed. It is not very comfortable sometimes, especially on cold mornings, but they might as well take it good natured, as they have to be there unless they are sick like myself.

Saturday, December 5, 1868

It is very cold and disagreeable this morning and I failed to show up at roll call. When the orderly came to see me I showed him my excuse. He smiled and said he had an easy job for me, but I told him I wasn't looking for work now. I had a job trying to keep warm as the wind was blowing hard and very cold. I did not stand or sit around the fire where the lieutenant could see me. I have another day yet and I am anxiously looking for Capt. Finch for I do want to win out, although I can not be company clerk unless I am detailed again.

We have to pack wood a considerable distance but burn it in one big fire instead of many small ones. Our "A" tents are much more comfortable than the little dog tents.

Sunday, December 6, 1868

When we woke this morning we were covered with snow for it had snowed nearly all night and the wind had blown it through the flaps until our beds were entirely covered. It had been hard on our horses although they were well covered with blankets, but had no shelter from the wind. We lost thirty-eight in our regiment and I have not heard how many were frozen in the Seventh.

This morning we were ordered to take the horses to the timber a mile from camp and along the river. We found a place where the timber was so dense we did not feel the wind. There was some good grazing in places, also plenty of good wood, so we were quite comfortable. I had brought some rations and a kettle, so we cooked and ate in the woods. We gave the horses a quart of corn and the best grazing we could find, so were busy all day.

I am taking the best care of my horse that I can. I keep him blanketed and pull grass so he can eat at night all he wants. None look any better. The hunters want me to loan him for hunting, but I refuse though they promise me the best steaks.

Monday, December 7, 1868

We stayed in the woods all night without tents, but had plenty of blankets and good wood for fire. The weather did not seem very cold and we sat around a good fire until nearly midnight.

Early in the morning orders came for us to come to camp, as we were going to go on a campaign against the Indians. Capt. Finch and the boys from Starvation Camp—as they named it—came in yesterday. They were hungrier than we were. They had hardly anything to eat as game was very scarce and for a few days they had nothing but berries and many of them became so constipated they did not dare to eat them, and as it was, they suffered much pain most of the time, day and night. When the wagon train arrived they were allowed to eat only a little at one time, three hours apart. Some did not sleep fearing they would miss their portion.

They ate their first square meal yesterday after their arrival in this camp. Some of them have had hardships almost unbelievable, eating the flesh of the horses too poor to travel, or prairie dogs and any kind of meat they could kill, and it was without salt or seasoning.

I have no fear of Lieut. Stoddard now for I know I can depend on Capt. Finch for he is like a brother to me and has told me to do what was right and he would see that I had fair play. Stoddard has a very overbearing disposition and feels that he should be our captain. He almost ignores Lieut. Tilton, but Tilton takes it all with good grace. I hear that Lieut. Tilton is to stay here with the boys who have lost their horses.

Gen. Sheridan is to go with the Seventh and the camp will be in command of Maj. Dimon of our regiment while Lieut. Gordon of Company H and Lieut. Tilton of Company L will have charge of train guards.

We are all excited getting ready to march. Each company has a wagon and provisions, blankets and dog tents.

We get started about noon and go up the river on the north side for twelve miles and cross to the south side and go into camp. There is very little timber here. We got to see Gen. Custer today at close range. He is of medium size, light complexion, long curly golden hair, wears a light colored hat and buckskin suit, the same as the scouts wear, with leather fringe on the seams of arms and legs. His men all like him.

Tuesday, December 8, 1868

Reveille at 4. We march at 6 toward the south, following the trail of the Seventh on their return from the fight on the Washita River last month.

I have been detailed as a flank patrol and ride on the left of the column. The patrols ride 150 yards apart and a quarter mile from the main line of troopers. The object is to discover any ambush by the Indians. The advance guard is composed of scouts and sharpshooters who cover a half mile in advance. The rear guard, having fifty or more, protect the wagon train from the rear and pick up stragglers and kill horses and mules that have given out and are unable to travel. We also have a pioneer corps in the advance who see that suitable crossings are made for the wagons.

When a very steep place is encountered the teams double up until several wagons are across, when wagons are fastened together and those across help pull those below the hill. We are fortunate to have good roads and crossings, as the roads have been made by the Seventh. Indians could easily kill a patrol and get away, but the risk has to be taken for protection to the troops. We have seen no Indians and do not expect to see any unless it would be a hunting party, or scouts watching our movements.

We camp on Hackberry Creek where there is very little timber, but plenty of driftwood. The stream is quite small. I do not have to cook and we have one of the mess to do it all, and we do his duty as guard, taking our turns.

It is quite cold tonight and we sleep in the open. I have only my own horse to graze and manage to find a blanket full of pretty good feed so he will have all he wants. The grass is dry and not much nutriment in it.

Wednesday, December 9, 1868

We are in our saddles by 6 o'clock and still follow the trail. I was so well pleased with my position yesterday that I obtained the same today. We have seen no timber since we left the Canadian, except the few scrubs along Hackberry Creek. The land here is very poor and looks like yellow clay. It is covered in places with scrub oak bushes, only a few inches high but have acorns on them.

We have only gone fifteen miles today and camp on the South Canadian in a bend of the river, where there is plenty of tall grass so our horses can have a good feed. They get a quart of corn every morning and graze at night.

We can see a high hill west of here and are told it is Antelope Hill. The river bottom seems to be very fertile and is over a mile wide and covered with dead grass a foot high. There is not much water in the channel although about 100 yards wide, but only a couple of inches deep. The sand bars would indicate a large stream at certain times. We pull enough dry grass to make us a comfortable bed. We are having pretty good rations on this trip, but some of the boys are not satisfied and are stealing officers' stores from the wagons. They get canned goods which are not issued to us.

Thursday, December 10, 1868

We had a very good bed last night and slept fine. We march at 6 as that seems to be the hour to be in our saddles. I ride with the company. I have no clerical work to do nor have any duty of my own only to relieve the cook when his turn comes.

Capt. Finch asked me how I would like to be detailed to go into the commissary department and help guard the wagons containing the provisions. He said they would rather feed a few guards than have their provisions all stolen. I told him I would go and try it awhile. Each company was to send a man who would be in charge of a duty sergeant who would detail a guard each day or night from the men under him.

I reported this evening for duty on my new position. There are twelve men in the detail and the sergeant is John W. Casebier from Company A. He selected three of us to go on guard and I am on guard for the first time since my enlistment. We are on duty two hours and off four for twenty-four hours, then relieved for two days. We ride with the company wagons or behind them.

Today we passed the place where the Seventh left their coats before going down into the Washita bottom to attack the Indian camp, and they discovered when they returned that their coats had been stolen by the Indians. The day has been very pleasant and we go into camp on the Washita about a mile from where the fight took place in the valley near the river.

Friday, December 11, 1868

We did not march today and all, who can leave, go over to the battle ground. About 8 o'clock the Seventh marched in line across to the river and most of our regiment following. There were perhaps a hundred stayed with the train.

As I was on duty I could not leave but was anxious to go. We were so new on our job we disliked to ask special favors this soon, so stayed and said nothing. We could visit our companies when not on duty, so this evening I went over and the boys told me what was done. They said it looked like there had been a considerable "mixup." The principal object of the visit by the troops was to find the bodies of Maj. Elliott and the men who were killed with him for they did not find them after the fight. They finally found the bodies nearly a quarter mile from the original camp. They must have been separated from the others by the Indians and forced farther away until all were killed. Their clothes were taken and their naked bodies fearfully gashed with knives and tomahawks. They were buried in a trench at the foot of a small mound. Major Elliott was buried separately on top of the mound with the men at his feet.

All the dead Indians were carried away by the others. Many of the squaws and children escaped during the fight because the orders were to spare the women and children and many warriors escaped by putting blankets over their heads like a squaw, and so made their escape. Indian men wear blankets over the left shoulder and under the right arm or diagonally over the back, so they took advantage of it.

One of the boys was shown where a little white boy was killed by a squaw who had him, and looking for a chance to get away, but when surrounded she plunged a knife into his heart and killed him, and was herself killed by those who witnessed the dastardly deed. Their bodies were not found today.

Saturday, December 12, 1868

It is snowing today and I am off duty and ride with the company. I hear more about the fight and how it looked on the battle ground. The bodies of the horses or ponies were scattered everywhere and the wolves for miles around will have a feed for some time. There are horses and mules killed every day as they are too poor and weak to travel. We are going down the river and our destination now is old Fort Cobb on this stream. It is called Washita River but it is not over ten feet wide in many places and is very crooked, so the wagons have to cross it quite often. The banks have to be dug down so the wagons can get across. We leave nothing the Indians can use, so we kill the weak animals.

We have passed several abandoned villages, for the frames of their tepees, made of willows, are left behind. There are pieces of broken saddles, broken lodge poles, pieces of canvas and blankets, so it is easy to tell where a camp has been. They build fires in holes and roast meat over the coals or barbecue it.

While Indian signs are plentiful we have not seen an Indian all day. They seem to have moved down stream, for the scouts say there are trails toward the southwest and part of them have gone that direction. We are anxious to meet some of them.

Sunday, December 13, 1868

Six o'clock seems to be the time when every man must be ready to march and the wagons fall in behind the column. Sometimes we come across the pioneer corps when they have a bad crossing to make or several close together,

but seldom have to wait long as they go before the column
and can call out for help if needed. We have to keep near
the river for the higher ground or bluffs have such deep ravines we could not cross them. We have concluded to camp
with the train instead of going to our companies every
night when off duty. Sergt. Casebier has to stay every
night to relieve the guard, so we will all stay with him.
We draw our rations as a mess and Sergt. Mather of the
commissary is pleased that we stay and says he will treat
us well for his orders are to give us plenty but to refuse any
who fail to keep watch of the wagons.

We have plenty of visitors from the companies and they
want to be very familiar and may be wanting to see how
close we guard the wagons. They ask if we care if they
come sometimes and spend the evenings. Sergt. Mather
says to have them stay away, but we can visit the company any time when not on duty. We think he is a pretty
nice fellow and help him whenever we can.

Monday, December 14, 1868

We stay with the train all the time now. We have
noticed signs of very recent fires left by the Indians, so they
cannot be very far from us. No doubt they have spies out
watching every move we make. This afternoon we have
seen two or three stray ponies that failed to get out of the
brush in time, for we must be close to them.

The Indians haul their goods on two poles about eighteen
feet long. The small ends are fastened like shafts on the
sides of a pony, one strap around the breast, the other
over his back. Behind the pony they are fastened together
with cross poles, close together so things will not fall
through. On these are placed tents, bedding, camp utensils,
squaws with babies and the aged too old to walk. Usually
the pony is led by the young boys or girls, but some will

follow the leader. They usually string out for a mile or two. When a pony sees a bunch of good grass he stops to eat unless led by some one.

While we all·eat in one mess we have four tents. They are of the "dog" variety and as long as the weather is not windy or cold we can get along pretty well, but if the wind blows hard and cold we dread to go on guard or even go to bed and sit around the fire until late.

Tuesday, December 15, 1868

My first experience came last night just after the boys had gone to bed. I thought I heard a noise and hurried to the rear of the last wagon, when I saw someone hurrying away with a box. I called to him to halt, when he dropped the box and crawled on his hands and knees over a bank and out of sight. It was part of a box of crackers he had taken from a wagon. He had slipped in and gotten into the wagon while the guards were being relieved and was not quite quick enough. I heard him or some one later in the dark and called to them to come in close or I would shoot. They did not come so I shot in their direction but did not hear anything more.

The river bottom keeps getting wider and we do not have to cross the stream so often, so get along pretty well but slowly as we have to rest quite often. We have gone fifteen miles today. The grazing is better now and the Indians have left the river as their trail is not to be seen any more. The command has stopped several times today and let their horses graze. The soil is pretty rich along the river with many large oak trees and less cottonwood and willow. I have a nice piece of tanned buffalo hide with long hair, which I picked up yesterday and some of the boys want to trade for it, but I will keep it.

SA-TAN-TA, PRINCIPAL WAR CHIEF OF THE KIOWA INDIANS

—From the Collection of E. A. Brininstool.

Wednesday, December 16, 1868

The wagons start out ahead of the command this morning but the advance guard, scouts and officers are always in advance. We have little use for the pioneer corps as the roads are very good and no streams to cross.

There are plenty of signs of Indians near us, so the troops keep close behind for we may expect an attack at any time. We have not seen a redskin since we left Camp Supply, although we have come a long way to make their acquaintance, but they are not even friendly. The scouts say they are not likely to attack us as their ponies are in very poor condition at this time of the year, but they might do so if they had their women and children where they would be safe.

We are going as fast as they are, so they left the river to get farther away, but will still keep watch on us that we do not follow too closely. We can see no signs of the poles being dragged as we could several days ago, but only pony tracks, so the families have very likely fallen out, going in another direction while we may meet those ahead at Fort Cobb when we arrive. We all ride with the wagons during the day and have to guard every third night.

Thursday, December 17, 1868

About 10 o'clock today a scout came in and said there were Indians in front bearing a flag of truce and wanted to talk to the Big White Chief. They were messengers from the Kiowa chiefs, Satanta and Lone Wolf. With the chiefs was a scout from Fort Cobb, who told our officers the Indians were holding another scout at their camp.

The Indians wanted a parley, but Gen. Custer was in favor of attacking them. Gen. Sheridan wanted to hear what they had to say, thinking perhaps it was possible to induce them to go on a reservation peaceably. After they had talked a while they agreed to release the scout and come to Fort Cobb and camp near the fort. Then Custer told the chiefs to stay with us until every Indian man, woman and child was in camp as they promised. Satanta made an effort to ride away but was told to halt or he would be shot. It was then he learned that we were down there to see that they were to be peaceable hereafter.

We have noticed a squaw riding in an ambulance with the Seventh and learned that it is Black Kettle's sister, Mahwissa, captured in the fight on November 27, who says she can get the Cheyennes to go on a reservation.

Friday, December 18, 1868

The scouts inform the command there are 3000 Indians within a few miles of us, all well armed with guns and most of them have one and two revolvers. They are making a great display of strength.

The scout who was held by the Indians tells us that it was their intention to get away but since the chiefs are not allowed to return they are awaiting further orders. Satanta's son is allowed to come in and take orders from the Big White Chief (Gen. Sheridan) as to what he wants them to do.

We reached Fort Cobb at dark and camped on the bank of the river near the fort or some other building that does not look very much like a fort. There are a good many Indians here already and we are told they are Comanches, but no Cheyennes as they went west or southwest after the fight with Black Kettle and were somewhere near the Wichita Mountains.

There is considerable timber around here, and the stream is wider. We are likely to stay here during the rest of our enlistment and see that Satanta complies with his agreement. Custer says he does not take an Indian's word for anything as he had learned last year that all of them were liars.

Saturday, December 19, 1868

Everyone is cleaning up for regimental inspection this afternoon. Our guns have to be polished, also buckles on straps and belts. We have to have clean clothes and boots to look as well as we can make them without polish. Some of the 7th Cavalry are expected to be there and Col. Crawford has given orders for every man to look as clean as soap and water can make him. We have to go to our companies and march out with them. I have spent most of the day cleaning and polishing, even going over saddle and bridle with a greasy woolen cloth. It happens that my suit is nearly new so I will average with the rest of the company.

Promptly at 2 o'clock we formed in battalions of three companies each on the parade ground and rode in front of the officers—Gens. Sheridan, Custer, Hazen and our regimental officers. About fifty feet to their right stood the Indian chiefs, Satanta, Lone Wolf of the Kiowas and Ten Bears, a Comanche chief. A son of Satanta was also with them. The Indians were on horseback and wore the chief's headdress of beads and feathers.

Satanta's son had on pants and shirt and a red and black blanket over his shoulders. He is his father's messenger and a fine looking boy, straight as an arrow and appears to be about 20 years old. Satanta is quite large and very strongly built, much more noble looking than the others who are darker and just ordinary looking Indians, only finely dressed.

Sunday, December 20, 1868

We are sleeping under the wagons and the train master is waiting for orders to unload, but have to wait until it is certain the Indians will come in and camp near here or whether we will have to go after them, so we just camp until we know.

There is no fort here, only a large warehouse and quarters for probably one or two companies. The warehouse contains hay, grain and Army supplies of all kinds, even wagons, tents and officers' beds and chairs. We do not get any of it, at least we have not seen anything yet. The officers have been issued a few tables and stools. Every few days a train comes in from Fort Arbuckle, farther down the river, with supplies for the Indians who have been coming for them while the warriors were up in Kansas killing settlers and carrying off the young women.

There is a sutler here who sells writing material and stamps to the soldiers and a mail comes in once a week and takes out the mail from here. All who have any money go to the sutler and get writing material and are writing letters to their friends at home. Letters are taken without stamps and sent collect. We have not been paid a cent since we left Kansas although the paymaster has paid the regulars. They say they have no orders to pay us anything, so cannot do so now. There is very little money in our whole regiment.

Monday, December 21, 1868

The train unloaded today, for the Indians are now coming in pretty fast and camping across the river about a mile above the fort. Most of the wagons went to Arbuckle in another train after supplies, for there are not only the soldiers but the Indians to feed. We have been issued supplies for ten days, and we have to guard them closely. They are piled under a big tarpaulin tent and there has to be a guard on both sides all the time. The officers' stores are stacked in the center row and the other provisions on either side.

One man of our company is missing and it is thought by some that he went in the wagon train to Arbuckle or followed it as his horse is also missing.

I lost my gold pen this evening and will have to use a pencil to keep my records and diary. I have gotten pretty well acquainted with all the men in our squad, all of them very nice fellows. Their names are John W. Casebier, Sergt.; A. Gustaf, Lewis Harriman, A. P. Ingleman, Duncan McCarty, W. T. Sloan, George Vann, George Warren, Stephen J. Van Dorn, Frank Van Horn, John Martin, Joseph Downing. All of them enlisted in different parts of Kansas. We have pretty good times together and those who command us are fine fellows. The Indians are making lots of noise and they are dancing and yelling until a late hour.

Tuesday, December 22, 1868

The Indians are not allowed to camp within a mile of us and we have to have a double line of pickets besides the camp guard. There are at least three Indians here now to one white soldier.

We drew new dog tents today and put them up near the big tents. We have the sides of the big tent taken off in fair weather so we can see that no one can get under the canvas without being seen by the sentry. My company is camped nearest to us, next to the river and on lower ground. We have put our tent on a high place where the water can run off if it rains. Three of us occupy one tent. My partners are Geo. W. Vann and A. P. Ingleman.

The whole regiment has dog tents and we do not like them at all as we have to get down on all fours to get inside.   The regulars have "A" tents like those of our officers while at the Seventh headquarters they have wall tents, about 12 x 20 feet.   It does not look to me that we Americans are all "born free and equal," but perhaps that does not apply to all soldiers.   We have to be satisfied with what we get, but is all they have here, and it is a protection from the weather, both rain and wind.

I have not heard from home since I left Kansas, and when I see others reading letters, with a smile on their faces, it makes me feel lonesome.   Were it not for the tricks we play on each other, our time would pass very slowly.

Our horses are beginning to look better with two feeds of corn daily and the grass we manage to find for them.

This afternoon six of my comrades and myself visited a Kiowa camp, near Fort Cobb.   The tents were widely scattered along the south bank of the Washita, sometimes three or four close together.   There were few Indians outside the tents except children.

We soon came to a group of boys who were playing a game with arrows.   They had two stakes about thirty feet apart.   They stood at one stake and threw their arrows with the hand, sticking them in the ground around the other stake.   It was very much like the white man pitches horseshoes.   They would put the arrows quite close so very few were more than a foot from the stake.   After a lot of Indian talk they would then pitch them back to the other stake.   While we were watching the game some dogs chased a squirrel up a tree a short distance away and began to bark when the boys left their game and went to the dog.

We could see the squirrel lying flat on the top of a large limb about forty feet from the ground.   Several boys were soon there with the bows and arrows.   One of them who seemed to be a good shot, sent an arrow so close

that the squirrel jumped higher on the limb and laid closer
than before. The same boy shot again and the arrow
plowed through the hair on his back. He ran out on a
small limb and jumped into space. He no sooner struck the
ground when one of the dogs seized him and ended the
sport.

We next visited a kind of work shop, where two or
three old men were making bridles, lariats, leggins and
some other things out of colored leather. The bridles were
made from tanned leather cut in strips and nicely braided,
and lariats were made in the same way. Moccasins and
leggins were trimmed with fringe on the seams. The
work was well done for the kind of tools they used. They
did not notice us or speak to us and when we spoke to
them they sometimes gave a grunt, but said nothing that
we could understand. We did not have any money, so did
not offer to buy anything.

There were no men to be seen except a few old ones, and
they all seemed to be busy. An old squaw came up to us
and offered to sell us a pair of nicely beaded moccasins.
She could not understand us, nor could she tell us the price.
She finally started off and motioned for us to follow, which
we did. She led us to a nice tent some distance, where the
lodges were quite thick, and there we met a very intelligent
looking squaw who could talk English. She was engaged in
making fancy work of scenery, buds and flowers, on cloth
and leather, and showed us some very gaudy clothing,
trimmed with many colored beads. She said she learned to
do that kind of work at an Indian School at some place in
Texas. She stayed there nearly five years, and learned to
do what we saw, and also learned to speak English. She
did not sell her work for money, but traders visited their
camp about once a month and she exchanged her goods
for what she wanted such as beads, thread, needles, cloth-

ing, purses and hand bags, which she trimmed and traded back again. She said the white men were very good to her and she would like to have her people become like those she had lived among for several years.

We visited another tent where two squaws were engaged in painting pictures. They had the walls of their tent covered with skins of various sizes and on each was a painting of some kind. On one that seemed most beautiful was a picture, in colors, of mountain scenery, a small lake, with an Indian village near the shore on one side. The two women occasionally spoke to each other, but said nothing to us and we went on to the next people we saw. An old squaw and two old men were making a frame of wicker work for an addition to their tepee. The frame was in the shape of a "prairie schooner" made of willows tied with leather. The sides were perpendicular for about four feet and then arched over, making a room 6 x 10. Another one near was finished and covered with buffalo skins. This was to be the bedroom to their home.

Then we returned and found the boys still near where we left them but they had bows and arrows and showed us some good markmanship with that kind of weapon. They could hit a circle three inches in diameter quite often at thirty feet, and some hit it at fifty feet or more.

When they tell you an Indian is lazy, we beg to dispute it, for we did not see one idle in all that camp. All were doing something, even the little youngsters.

Wednesday, December 23, 1868

There is not much doing in camp today and the boys in the company are hatching up an idea to create some excitement. Our great want is more room in our tent, so we conclude to dig a square hole, the size of our tent, deep enough so we can stand. On one side we dig the floor six or eight inches deeper and make our bed on the higher portion. Tomorrow we will make a fireplace in the side where the floor is low and then we can sit on our bed before the fire.

We will not have to hunt so much wood nor have such a big fire to keep warm. Nearly all the company have begun making dugouts, or will do so. It is a great protection from the weather and much more comfortable. We have an arrangement that one of us is on duty each night, so we have fire all night and also have more room in our tent.

Thursday, December 24, 1868

Our fireplace is a good idea so we spend much of our time inside lying on our beds. We cook our meals inside now and use a wide box lid for a table. Many of the company boys have been to see our new home and have the "idea." Many of them are hard at it and will soon be comfortable. Our chimney draws nicely and we are not troubled with smoke. While out grazing our horses today we pulled enough dead grass to make a much softer bed than the one we had last night.

Our fire makes enough light that we could read if we had anything to read, so one of the boys in the squad got a deck of cards somewhere and we borrowed them and play once in a while. I do not know any of the games except euchre but Ingleman is a pretty good player and knows several games. One is what he calls seven-up—also cribbage. I think I will like the last game, but he says it requires a counter, but he will make one and then I can learn it.

This is Christmas Eve and we lie on our bed and tell what we would likely be doing if we were at home. I told them I would very likely be at some church's Christmas tree and have a good time.

Friday, December 25, 1868

Merry Christmas! It is a very cold day and it is my turn to stand guard. The wind is blowing a hurricane from the north and we have the sides up around the big tent so it is a protection to our dog tent which is about twenty feet south. Several of the tents in my company have been torn loose by the wind and the boys are pounding stakes to make them more secure. It so happens we have very little provisions in the commissary and I can get inside and on top of a pile of boxes where I can see everywhere inside, so I asked Sergt. Mather if I can sit up there and watch things. He told me "All right," so I am protected from the wind and is so much more comfortable, besides it requires only one man and we do not get so cold.

We surely enjoy sitting by our fireplace today. When I am off duty I write letters to my home folks and to some of my schoolmates. Sergt. Mather came in today to see how we were and was very much pleased that we were so comfortable. Sergt. Casebier has not "lived" with us, but goes to his company except to relieve us. The other boys have three tents and are fixed nearly as well as we are, only one has a fireplace yet.

Saturday, December 26, 1868

There is a great change in the weather today, to a warm and pleasant one. As I am off duty I do my washing for I have plenty of soap and will likely have to go on inspection again tomorrow, for it is the only church we have when the whole regiment attends. We try to keep pretty clean when we can do so, as we have to salute our officers when they come our way.

George Vann and I have become pretty good friends. He is several years older than I and has a claim about thirty miles from Junction City. His wife and baby have gone

east to spend the winter. It has become unsafe to be so
far from civilization on account of Indians. Her folks sent
her money to go back east, so she took her little boy and
left to stay until spring. He got so lonesome he concluded
to enlist for six months and perhaps by that time it
would be safe for his wife and baby to return.

Gus Ingleman is about my age and his home is near
Lawrence. He is from Company F, while George Vann is
from Company K. I have not learned much about the
other members of the squad only their companies. Casebier is from Company A, and a nice-looking young fellow.

Sunday, December 27, 1868

I did not have to go to inspection today as those detailed
for guard duty are excused. Some of the boys did not have
their guns very clean, or their clothes or faces, and hands
were not up to the test and were sent to the guard house
and were made to clean up later. There is a man in our
company who seldom washes even hands and face and he
was told to clean up, or the guard would have to do it for
him, and they need not be very careful how much they
hurt him.

I have plenty of time today between post hours to write
letters, and we get our writing material of the sutler over
at the post where he has quite a little store. My money
is nearly gone, less than a dollar, but all I need money for
is to buy paper, envelopes and stamps.

We cannot understand why we do not get our pay when
the paymaster comes and pays the regulars every month,
but passes us every time.

The regimental commissary is Lieut. John Johnston, and
the commissary sergeant is William Mather. Lieut. Johnston is quite friendly and talks with us, but not so confiden-
tially or kindly as Sergt. Mather. Sometimes when we go

for our rations Mather says do this or that to help him, and he always gives us extra. He has asked me several times to "tend store" for him when he went on errands.

Monday, December 28, 1868

It is very cloudy all day and tonight. We have drawn ten days' rations for the regiment and we have to put a sentry outside the tent which is filled with provisions for the men and grain for the horses and mules.

Francis M. Brown is the quartermaster sergeant and issues the feed from the tent twice a day. Luther A. Thresher is the regimental quartermaster. While the feed is in one end and the provisions in the other end of the tent we have to guard both ends, which is no more than we have done before.

I have been over to the sutler's and post office to mail my letters. We pay five cents for a stamp. Most of the boys get their stamps with the letters. Joe Downing of our squad always gets paper and stamped envelopes with his letters so he can answer his letters any time. I have not even had a letter yet, but perhaps no one back home knows how to get a letter to me, so they don't write. We have been on the move so much I doubt if the Government knows just where to find us all the time. I have heard nothing yet what we are expected to do next. The Indians are all camped across the river and Satanta and Lone Wolf have been released.

Tuesday, December 29, 1868

It is raining today and the boys are standing under the big tent, each so they can see anyone coming from any direction. Mather sees that we have our duty as pleasant as possible and we appreciate it, so try in every way to repay

LONE WOLF, A NOTED WAR CHIEF OF THE KIOWA INDIANS
—From the Collection of E. A. Brininstool.

him by helping him when he needs it, so he can see we appreciate his kindness.

We had to dig small ditches under the edge of our dog tent so the water would run off. As the tent is on a hill the water does not run inside. Tonight the ground has become so saturated with water that it seeps in and runs down the walls. We then dig a narrow ditch near the wall around our bed so the water can run toward the side of the fireplace, where we have a hole several inches deep, and we dip the water into a kettle when it gets full.

When the sentry changes, he dips out the water and empties it outside, so we still keep dry but it is raining very hard outside. Sometimes we do not go to bed until quite late and we hear the boys over at the company so they must be having a great time. We joke and tell stories until we get sleepy. Lieut. Johnston told us we could use the empty boxes for fuel, so they take the place of the wet wood that we would have to go and get in the rain.

Wednesday, December 30, 1868

It is still raining and we still have to dip water. We hope it will not get so soaked, so the ground will cave in. The camp is nearly all under water and when we got up this morning the camp of my company was deserted and the tents gone. All we could see was a row of holes full of water. The water came into their tents in the night and they had to get out of bed and grab bed, clothing and tents and hunt for higher ground.

They went about half a mile to the timber and built a great fire, which made it light enough to see to put up their tents again, but they were nearly frozen before they had a fire, and everything so wet they could not go to bed. The ground is so soft that there is mud everywhere. I go over to the woods to see the boys and find them around big fires drying their clothes and bedding.

We have changed the hours of guard duty. Instead of all day and all night we change after 12 hours, so I go on every other day and every other night, instead of every fourth day. We are only trying it out, but we will have a change and may go back to the old way again.

Thursday, December 31, 1868

It has stopped raining but is still cloudy. We have no water coming in our tent today, but it is very muddy outside and we have to clean our shoes before we can go inside. We surely will have a fireplace whenever we camp at any place for any length of time. We cook our meals, sit by the fire and eat.

The boys all came back to camp today and mustered for pay. There were some who did not answer when their names were called. They were a hard-looking lot of men and some of them had some of their dugout mud on them yet. The sutler will have to send for a new stock of goods if we get our pay. Most of the men need new clothing and boots, for they are getting ragged and barefooted. My boots leak some if I get in the water. They are the ones I bought in Springhill, when I enlisted. They were all the citizens' clothing I kept. We are expecting a train in every day with supplies for they were to be here in ten days from the time they left here. We hear nothing more about going after Indians for the Kiowas have done as they agreed and we may not have to go any further. But would like to have a pay day pretty soon.

Friday, January 1, 1869

It is still cloudy this morning and even if it does not rain the camp is not liable to be occupied again. The company is still in the woods but there is no formation as tents are scattered all around, for every one put his tent where he could find a suitable place.

We had quite an excitement soon after dark. Some one threw a lot of cartridges in the fire and they began to explode when some one yelled, "The Indians are coming!" Then the bugles began to call to arms and we could hear the order to "Fall in!" The Seventh bugles also sounded and shortly two troops came galloping toward our regiment, but it was all a scare and no one was hurt. Had the Indians known it they would have said, "Much scared."

We get very little corn for our herds but I get two feeds a day yet, as I have free access to the quartermaster's stores.

Our squad has our horses staked out by lariats and one of us goes out at noon to water and change them to better grazing. While we left all the men that had lost their horses at Camp Supply, there are several more in our company who would have to walk if we should have to march again.

We hear from some of the clerks at our headquarters that the Regulars are going out after the Cheyennes and we may have to go along. The Cheyennes are the ones that have given the trouble in Kansas and they are all still off their reservations and will have to be brought in.

Saturday, January 2, 1869

The regiment has gone into camp in regular order again, the companies in lines one half mile down the river, and on higher ground where there is no danger from floods.

We expect to move the big tent and all its contents down to headquarters and we will have to leave our dugouts and all our comforts. We can make a better one next time if we stay long enough in one place. There is quite a distance between the two regiments now and we see very little of each other. I have not seen a Regular officer for a week.

The boys tell a joke on Lieut. Stoddard: that in the excitement last night he came running down among the boys crying "Fall in! Fall in! Every man with nine loads in his carbine"—and the magazine only holds seven. He and I speak when we meet, but perhaps if he had the opportunity he would get me into trouble. He knows there are a number of the boys who do not like him very well and he seldom comes down and speaks to them.

Capt. Finch is different—he often comes down the lines and jokes with them and tells them if any of them are treated badly or different from the others, to report it to him and he will see that all fare alike. While Lieut. Tilton was with us he was a boy among us, and all seemed to like him. The boys who knew him in Paola say he was liked by all who knew him.

Sunday, January 3, 1869

We moved the commissary over near our headquarters and have a very pleasant location and pick out a high place for our tent where the water will run off instead of inside. This can be made a fine camp and both wood and water are near. When we go down to the river we can see the Indian camp about a mile below us and there are more above but out of sight. Those above are Kiowas and those below are part of the Comanches. They are not allowed to graze their ponies on our side of the river, nor are we allowed to cross to their side, and we are peaceable neighbors. They do not visit us and we are not allowed to visit them, but we would like to go over sometime and see how they live.

The feed is not very good for our horses and we may move down the river a few miles or some place where there is better grazing. All the grass is dead and has been exposed to the winter weather, so there is no nutriment in it, and stock would never get in good condition if they had plenty of it.

Two or three of us have to stay with the horses now and it keeps me busy finding something the horses will eat. We have had no grain for several days. Most of the horses are pretty weak.

Monday, January 4, 1869

We have orders to move this morning and everyone is busy getting his belongings together to put in the wagons. A large wagon train came in from Arbuckle last night and several wagons will go with us and will not be unloaded until we find a camp suitable for our needs.

We are ready to march by noon and go about ten miles west and after finding a good camp location it is eight o'clock and dark, but we soon have a fire and bacon frying. There is plenty of wood and water on all the creeks in this part of the country so have no trouble in finding a good camping place. We have left the Washita, and can see the Wichita Mountains from any elevated place.

Our mules are so weak we can haul only a part of a load in each wagon and when we come to a muddy or sandy place they can't pull the load and they have to double teams, until the place is crossed. So much time is lost that we have time to graze our horses at every stop. The train men have to work now and say we have a "lazy job."

We walk along beside the train and talk with the teamsters. Some of them are like ourselves, out here to see sights and get some experience to relate when they get back home.

Tuesday, January 5, 1869

We are all ready to start by daylight, but many of the mules are in such poor condition that they can hardly walk, without pulling anything. We soon strike a miry place about half a mile wide and the men have to pry up the wheels and pack dead grass and sticks or brush under them. After two or three hours' hard work a lot of men are detailed to cut and pack brush for a road across the soft places. It has been a very slow and hard task for everybody as well as for the mules.

We only went five miles all day, but have gotten to higher ground and everybody is glad, for another day like this would incur the loss of nearly the whole train. Some of the boys with the trains are singing "This Is a Hard Road to Travel." The wagon train has been favored with a nice camping place on high ground with plenty of wood and water. Every mule is given a quart of corn and some hay. The cavalry has to go without either. The teamsters have mess boxes in each wagon and never start on a trip unless it is filled with plenty of provisions for the trip. They don't have to draw rations like the rest of us, and they usually have plenty to eat every day and all the time.

Wednesday, January 6, 1869

We are on the march at sunrise and have no miry roads or places to cross, but after going ten miles we come to a good camping place and plenty of feed where we stop and draw rations and clothing, making the wagons lighter for the mules. Everyone has plenty to eat and wear now so there is no complaint even from the "growlers."

We still have to guard our supply train as some of the men would eat officers' stores of canned goods, if they had a chance to get them. The quartermaster's train goes ahead of ours and the company wagons in the rear. We all guard our train during the march by riding with it, and as soon as we go into camp a guard is put on. We have no sergeant with us now as Casebier has gone back to his company and we make our hours of duty and go on in regular rotation. We always sleep near the wagons or under them, so when the time comes to change, the one on duty wakes the next man and he relieves him. We have no trouble among ourselves, and our plan works well. The wagon train of the Regulars is larger than ours, and always goes in advance of our regiment while ours is always in the rear. Each train has a "wagon boss" or train master who sees to everything and gives orders to the teamsters. They won't allow any of the foot soldiers to ride in the wagons.

Thursday, January 7, 1869

The scouts have found a beautiful camping spot, a couple of miles ahead where there is plenty of wood, water and grass, so we move on to it, but it began to rain soon and we had to put up our tents in the rain. The timber here is of several kinds, with a good many pecans. We find many nuts among the leaves, some mouldy but many good ones, only wet. Our mess found all we could eat, but had to dry them first. Our tent is under a large pecan tree and we had gotten a good many nuts before the other boys knew of them. We have plenty of dry wood and a good fire.

We may stay here some time for the camp is an ideal one for all concerned. When not marching, guards go on duty watching the wagons. We have seen no Indians since we left Cobb, but have pickets out nearly a mile from the camp. I am glad I do not have to go out there and stand two hours in the rain and cold. At night the pickets are not allowed to build a fire and they don't know when an Indian might slip up in the dark and tomahawk them.

We have had a few pretty warm days and the green grass is coming up. No one seems to know how long we are to stay here. The Seventh still has the Indian squaw. She rides with the driver in an ambulance, although she sits on the floor.

Friday, January 8, 1869

We do not march today and I am off duty, so George Vann and I go up the creek as far as the pickets will let us. We get up on top of a hill where the picket stands and we can see a mountain or high hill that appears to be four or five miles distant. I have never been on a mountain, so I proposed to George that we go over to it if we can get a pass.

I went to see Adjt. Steele and he gave us a pass and after walking pretty fast for two hours the hill was as far as when we started—or seemed so. After going another mile we gave it up and went back to camp.

Vann shot a coyote on the way back. I had never seen one dead and it looked like a dog to me. It was after sundown when we got back to camp. The boys had a joke on us for they said that the hill was no less than twenty miles away. We had a change from guard duty and were not sorry we went. The day has been warm and pleasant.

The creek on which we are camped is called Cache Creek and is a tributary of the main Red River. We could see a wide strip of timber to the west extending north and southwest of the mountain. Most of the timber here is oak with some other kind near the creek. What we have seen of the soil around here would make splendid farming land for it is a rich sandy loam and near the creek it is black and covered with dead sunflowers.

Saturday, January 9, 1869

This is another pleasant day and wash day for the boys, for they are likely to have to be called out for inspection as we usually do every Sunday. I had just gotten my clothes ready to dry when Lieut. Johnston sent his orderly to tell us we could go to our companies tomorrow for inspection, so I spend the afternoon cleaning my gun and belt buckles until they shine.

Afterward Ingleman and I go to a hill near camp where we can see the mountain we started for yesterday and it looked much farther away. I think it must be one of the Wichita Mountains. It has no trees on it except at the base on the west side where a line of timber extends south toward this creek and may be a good sized stream.

Sunday, January 10, 1869

We march several miles today down the creek. The grazing is even better here as another creek nearly as large as Cache Creek empties into it from the west and we are in a wide valley where the grass is two feet tall and not entirely dead in some places. We can see the mountains plainly now. Our camp is on the bank of the creek flowing from the mountains, and the bank is ten feet or more higher than the stream, which is twenty feet wide and runs swiftly.

There is a large hill just opposite our camp and across the stream, nearly 100 feet high, and we can see small pines on the sides and on top. Along the bank across the creek is a thick patch of sweet briers, so we cannot cross. Our bank has no underbrush and is covered with tall grass. We have never seen such a beautiful place anywhere on our trip. We are in hopes we will get to stay here the rest of the winter. There is plenty of wood, water and grass. Now our only anxiety and worry will be to get something to eat for ourselves as the horses are pretty well provided for, if we can stay a month for the green feed will be plentiful here by that time.

Monday, January 11, 1869

Everything is quiet today and we have no orders of any kind. Ingleman and I went across the creek and explored the mountain over there. We took our guns as we did not know but we might need them. There are turkeys, quail and rabbits and there may be deer but we saw none. Gus killed a turkey and a pheasant as he saw both at the same time. They were quite tame so when he shot they did not fly away. We then built a fire and dressed the pheasant and roasted it for our lunch. I had some salt and it came in just right. I have a pocket in my blouse made on purpose to carry salt whenever I can get enough to fill it.

I had a fresh experience on the way to Camp Supply so I do not want to have another if I can help it. After we had eaten we were going down into a ravine when Gus saw a deer and shot at it. I heard it in the brush as it came toward me but I was excited and did not hit him either. He was soon out of sight. We were not expecting to see any deer and did not aim low enough. We sat down until we were steady and then we began looking for big game but did not see any deer, turkeys or quail.

Tuesday, January 12, 1869

Everybody has to stay in camp two days. We have inspection again and I suppose it is to keep us busy for it is so nice here everybody is getting restless. So many have been getting outside that guards are stationed close all around the camp with orders to let none get outside without a pass. There are pickets on all the hills within two miles of the camp for we are supposed to be in the Indian country. It is said the Comanches have a large camp on Cache Creek near the main Red River and claim all the country along Cache Creek. The pickets on the hills are to keep a lookout for Indians, but none have been seen yet. We have to keep two men on guard at night, but only one during the day. We have heard of no one trying to steal provisions for a long time, and Sergt. Mather says he has never missed anything and has told us several times that we were all right and he could trust every one of us.

We have been told there is another creek called Slough Creek a mile below where everything is good as it is here and we may move down there shortly.

William Sibbitt of our company died last night and we all turned out and buried him with honors of war. The doctor said, "Homesickness was the most that was the matter with him." He called all the time for his mother.

Wednesday, January 13, 1869

We pulled up camp this morning and moved over to Slough Creek and camped between two high hills, one of which is the one across from our last camp. We crossed over the creek and went to the other side of the hill. Cache Creek flows south and Slough Creek east, so we are camped on Slough Creek, one half mile from Cache on the west side toward Wichita Mountains. It is an ideal spot for the hillsides are covered with small pines. It is raining nearly all day and often pretty hard. We cannot imagine why we have to move in the rain, and not wait for more pleasant weather, but we put up our tents and carry wet wood to make our fires and cook our meals.

What hurts the worst is I have to go on duty tonight with wet clothing and it is blowing cold from the north. I get under the tarpaulin and on top of the boxes to keep out of the wind. I think I could hear anyone if they came inside even if it is dark. Everyone else got as wet as I, so there is not much danger of anyone coming to steal provisions. I told Mather I would go inside after tattoo, and he said go ahead and I did. He does all he can for us when we get in hard luck.

Thursday, January 14, 1869

It is cold and cloudy this morning. We sit by the fire and tell some of the experiences of our lives and jokes on the other people. One of the boys in Company K killed a deer yesterday and brought a nice piece to George Vann, so we had venison for our dinner. I got a pass to go hunting for Vann and me, so we go to the mountains about three miles from camp. We had hardly gotten there when a rabbit started up and ran behind some bushes. Vann told me to go on one side and he went on the other but I had not gone far when he shot and I went around and found he had already killed a deer. We went no further but got a long stick and carried it between us to camp. Now we had venison again for supper, but gave some to Adjt. Steel and Captain Finch, and George took a quarter to his company. We divided with the other boys and Sergt. Mather, giving him the best. Adjt. Steel came over and thanked us for the meat and told us whenever we wanted a pass to go again we could have it. I want to try it again and perhaps I will be lucky to get a deer.

Lieut. Stoddard has been quite friendly lately—maybe he has gotten a smell of venison! We saw several turkeys on the hill and I think they will not be very hard to kill. Vann and I are planning to go out when the moon is overhead and kill them by moonlight as the trees are only thirty or forty feet high in the foothills where they roost.

Friday, January 15, 1869

It is still cloudy and cold. We are protected by the hills from the wind. The trees along the creek protect us from the north. We are likely to stay here for some time as the camp is all that we can desire, and we are near enough to the Indians as long as they are peaceable.

Two noted Indian chiefs are visiting the Big Chief (Gen. Sheridan). They are Little Raven of the Arapahoes and Little Robe of the Cheyennes. They wanted to know why we are down here in their country. They were told that Uncle Sam wants them to go on a reservation and be peaceable. They would be fed and clothed. They were willing to do so as long as they were given plenty of food and clothing and blankets. Gen. Custer proposed to go back to the tribes with them to see how many there were in each tribe, but after they were on a reservation they must not leave without permission from the agent from the nearest fort.

Gen. Custer has taken about forty of his picked sharp-shooters to visit all the tribes that have not come in yet. There are some of each tribe that are not willing to go on the reservations. They want to be free to go anywhere they choose. Custer will take Mahwissa, the Cheyenne squaw and sister of Black Kettle, with him and deliver her to her tribe. He has learned much of the Indian feeling from her.

Gen. Sheridan is still with us and when Custer proposed to visit the Indian camp he told him he would not advise or order him to go nor would he oppose him. Many think it is extremely hazardous for him to go into a Cheyenne camp so soon after his fight with the Black Kettle band. He told them that was why he was taking Mahwissa as he had made her understand that he was always the friend of good Indians and the attack on their tribe was to stop the murder of white settlers by the Cheyennes.

We have seen Gen. Sheridan lately, as he has visited Col. Crawford's tent. He and Col. Crawford have been friends ever since he has been in command of this department. Governor Crawford offered to furnish a regiment to help him compel the Indians to be peaceable, so our regiment was a *gift* to the Government, and this is how we are appreciated! We have been only half fed and clothed for three months and the paymaster had ignored us several times so we are half fed and "dead broke" and most of us have to walk hundreds of miles from civilization. The Regulars are not treated that way, for those we have met do not complain.

Gen. Sheridan is a short, heavily built man, wears a dark blue suit, but not much gold out here. He passed when I was on duty and answered my salute. He is quite jovial and does not put on much style.

Saturday, January 16, 1869

It is clear this morning, but windy. We have plenty to eat now, but short on tobacco, and the men who use it are complaining because none was issued. I am glad I do not use it. I have never drawn any tobacco, although I am entitled to it and can have it, so I will take my portion of it next time and give to those of my friends who do use it. I saw a man give his note of $2.50 for a piece less than two inches square, payable at first pay day. That must be an expensive luxury, and I hope I will not be inclined to learn to chew.

Some of us are going up on the nearest hill tomorrow, so we can get a good view of the country for miles, except west, as the mountains are in that direction.

Sergt. Mather has made us a proposition that we take axes and go with the teams that he will furnish and get a load of good dry wood for fires for all of us, so we accept as it beats carrying wood for one fourth a mile or more as we have been doing lately. We have several dead trees in mind that will burn better than what we have been getting.

I help him weigh out the rations to be issued to the companies so they will be ready when they come for them. When we get ours he says, to take all we need but not to waste any.

Sunday, January 17, 1869

It is a beautiful day and the regiment has inspection. If anything happens that we can not turn out, we are inspected very soon after. That means clean clothes, clean faces and hands, bright guns and buckles. Our squad has not been ordered out but we prepared for it just the same.

We waded the creek this afternoon and climbed up on top of one of the hills where we could look down on our camp and also see the camp of the Seventh about two miles south of us, near Cache Creek. We are on Slough Creek and their camp is below or south.

There are a good many small pines on this hill but no brush on the top. The grass is about an inch high and green. We lie under a pine tree and listen to the wind blowing through the pines. It is my first experience in a pine forest. All the higher mountains are covered with pines and thick brush at their base. Between the hills are oak trees scattered so they are not close together. I can imagine this would be a lovely place for a home sometime. There is plenty of water and rich soil in the valleys. The most beautiful scenery I ever saw. I hope we will remain here until we are ready to go home, and then I shall always remember this place.

We hear this evening there will soon be a fort built on this creek and the tribes in this section will have reservations near, when it will be the supply station for them to draw food and clothing. As this is a part of the Indian territory it is not likely that the white man will ever have a chance to own a home here.

This afternoon some of the boys went up on a hill and saw several rattlesnakes on a large pile of rocks. They killed them with stones and then pried the rocks loose and rolled them down the hill. They pried a large rock loose and under it was a lot of snakes of all sizes, then they began a snake hunt. The result was they counted 103 dead snakes, many of them quite large. Later they brought them to camp, skinned them and put their belts through the skin so there are a lot of rattlesnake belts in camp tonight.

We are planning another hunt soon so we can explore the mountains to the west of our camp. They seem to be much higher than these near us with larger trees except those below the pines. The boys are very anxious that someone go up to the hills for meat. None of the other messes care to hunt so it will fall to us. I want to get up in the big pines again.

Monday, January 18, 1869

It is clear this morning and the sun is shining brightly and just the right kind of a day to go hunting. I called at the adjutant's tent and got a pass for George Vann and myself so we will go to the mountains. We went up the south side of the creek until we came to a place that looked like good hunting grounds when I saw a pheasant— or grouse, as Vann called it—and shot it. We soon came to a small stream and stopped and cleaned our bird and had it for our dinner for we brought a small frying pan along with which to cook our meat. We first fried it until done. We had hardtack for bread, but we surely enjoyed our meal.

We are going to stay all night in the hills and hunt turkeys by moonlight for the moon will be nearly overhead at 9 or 10 o'clock, so if we can find the roosting place we will have some turkey for our breakfast. We have a nice camp here, so gather a lot of dry wood for our fire tonight. We loaf around here and listen for the turkeys to come in to their roosting. It is almost as light as day and we can see overhead very plainly.

It was getting pretty dark and we began to think our turkey hunt was going to be a failure, but just then we heard them coming in, and they stopped some distance away, so we made a note of the direction and waited an hour or more, but finished our supper on what remained of our dinner. About nine o'clock the moon was well up and we started out.

We were about fifty feet apart looking for turkeys when Vann shot and just then something hit me on the shoulder. I had just been thinking what I would do if we ran across Indians, so I was not thinking of turkeys and when I was hit I jumped "so high"—and came down on the turkey!

We had pretty good luck as only a few of them flew after we would shoot. We had seven and they were as much as we could well carry. We left a good fire so we could find our way back to camp. I could only carry three but Vann was larger and stronger and walked faster than I could. We pulled them and hung them on a pole between two bushes. Then we got ready to turn in. We could hear a wolf somewhere howling and Vann said he smelled blood and would be near us before morning. He was still howling when we went to sleep.

Tuesday, January 19, 1869

When we waked this morning the sun was up and shining through the trees and about two hours high. As we had only our overcoats we slept with all our clothes on beside the fire. Once I woke up and a burning stick had fallen at my elbow and had burned through my overcoat and blouse and was getting to my arm. I put out the fire in my clothing, put on more wood and went to sleep again, as though I had not been on fire.

While George was getting our breakfast I took a walk around a hill to look for game when I came upon a deer feeding. He ran to the edge of a thicket near, and then stopped and looked at me in surprise. I was as much or more surprised than he for I was some time getting a good aim on him, but finally shot and he jumped in the brush. I thought he was gone, but I would go and see if I could see blood, but instead I found the dead deer. He only weighed about fifty pounds so I carried him back to camp, when we had our breakfast of fried turkey.

About ten o'clock we started for a little hunt before going to camp and leave our turkeys hanging until our return. After hunting an hour we returned to camp and we each had a deer. The one I killed had horns with two prongs.

We now had more than we could carry and Vann proposed that I go to camp and have Mather send a wagon out for them while he would try and add more to our store. On my way to camp I saw plenty of game, but too far to shoot and I was to hurry so kept on my way to camp. Just before I came to the creek I saw a horse and when I got close I saw it was my own which had pulled his picket pin and wandered away. I caught him and went back to the mountains and found George waiting. He had seen me

coming and had the turkeys tied with some string he had
brought. We used the lariat to tie the legs of the deer so
when we were ready to start we had the horse well loaded,
two deer on one side and deer and turkeys on the other
and carried a couple of turkeys on a pole between us.

When we got to camp there was a big crowd to meet
us. We took our load to Mather's tent and there divided
it. We gave our company officers a turkey and sent some
venison to headquarters, so Col. Crawford sent a "Thank
you" note signed by the regimental officers, and some to
non-commissioned officers. Our officers were remembered
and I took Frank and Bill some turkey and venison and Bill
asked if it was good to eat.

Wednesday, January 20, 1869

The first we heard this morning was a call to breakfast, "Fried venison with gravy, hot coffee and hardtack."
It is cloudy today and raining at times, but we are pretty
well supplied with food and clothing, a good camp and we
are kept busy most of the time. In the companies they are
getting up an interest in baseball and may soon form a
league, and in that way the companies will get to know
each other. Before coming here I did not know any one
outside of my own company except the officers who came to
call on ours. Now I am coming in contact with all of them,
even our regimental officers, and their orderlies and
clerks come to our big fire every night. They usually have
some news that they have heard from their superiors and
I often get information for my diary that the boys in the
companies never know.

I now weigh more than I ever have, 147 pounds, and my
usual weight is 130 to 135 pounds. I went over to the company this afternoon and the boys wanted to know all

about our hunt, and some of them say they are going if they have to crawl by the guard. It is almost impossible to get by with a gun and very few can get a pass.

Our wagons have to go to the Seventh's supply train for our rations and some of the boys hide in the wagons until outside and then go hunting. We saw where others had camped because there were pieces of hard tack, so it wasn't Indians.

Thursday, January 21, 1869

It is still cloudy but warm and we still have venison for breakfast and turkey for dinner, but it will not last much longer, when we will have to go back to sowbelly and hardtack. A train came in today with provisions from Fort Arbuckle. The picket saw them go to the Seventh's camp and we may get some rice and beans for a change.

I am in need of shoes for my toes are exposed and my socks have partly disappeared. The clothing is issued to the companies and I will have to go and get my share. There is not enough to supply every man, so they will go to those who are in the worst need. I was on duty when the distribution took place and when I did get there all that was left of the boots was a pair of 11's and I wear only 7's, but I had to take them or go barefoot.

I paraded around camp with my No. 11's awhile and told the boys if any of them had boots too small I would trade if they would give me enough. That offer was soon to be taken, for several had sizes too small and it was not long until I had a pretty good fit. It was pretty much the same with my blouse, but made only one trade.

We have had no mail for a long time, but if a fort is to be built near here we will have our mail regularly, but have no paper or envelopes.

Friday, January 22, 1869

We heard that the fort will be built on Cache Creek, a few miles below the Seventh's camp, and that the 10th Infantry, a colored regiment, will be stationed there until it is completed. The Seventh's officers are going to call it Fort Elliott in honor of Maj. Elliott, who was killed last November on the Washita in the fight with Black Kettle. I do not know who has the authority to give it a name, but the Seventh have proposed it.

I had quite a confidential visit today with Steve Van Dorn. He is from Company E, and has had quite an experience. He was first sergeant and had some trouble with Lieut. Brady, and was returned to sergeant, but a short time after he was reduced to the ranks, and when a man was asked to go into the commissary department, Capt. Darling sent him here. He appeared to be a very nice fellow, has a high school education. Lieut. Brady is a West Pointer, and is pretty domineering and a trial to Capt. Darling even if he is second lieutenant.

Company E is on the right of my Company L and Company A on the left. The officers run back and forth many times a day. I go over to Capt. Finch's nearly every day and meet them there. Capts. Pliley and Finch are becoming great "cronies" for they are together much of the time.

Saturday, January 23, 1869

We are having very pleasant weather now and the boys are getting restless. A few of them think they can put up a good ball game today at 2 o'clock. Corp. Studabecker was sent to the ranks today for refusal to obey Lieut. Stoddard and talking disrespectfully to him. We have to treat all officers respectfully even if we do not like them.

The ball used in the game today is made of yarn, with something inside to give it weight. It is covered with a piece of leather from an old boot. I think everybody is going to see the game as it is the first between the companies.

I do not know the rules, but Company L was winner, 7 to 2, but Company A claimed the umpire was not fair to them. He was from Company H but said he knew the rules and they got all that was coming to them. It has given the boys something to talk about and the "grumblers" have forgotten their complaints. Our boys have a challenge from Company E now and I suppose they will have to play all the companies until beaten and so on as long as they care to play ball, or leave for home in the spring.

Sunday, January 24, 1869

It is almost like summer today and we have no fire except to cook with. The bugler calls the boys out for inspection. Our company bugler is Rolla R. Watt, and he is one of the best, some say better than the chief bugler, William Gruber. All the buglers go to practice every afternoon. They have prepared a place around the hill so we cannot hear them in camp unless the wind comes from that direction.

Our rations are getting quite low again and we will have to go down to the Seventh's camp for more. Wagon trains are coming every day now, bringing material for the new fort and we may have to go there for our supplies. We all seem to have good health and Dr. Bailey says there are no men who have to stay at the hospital though several are coming at sick call, but no one is very sick. Our fresh meat is all gone and I would like 'to go for a hunt again. Some of the boys who were out did not have good success.

Monday, January 25, 1869

I go with Sergt. Mather today for rations. We did not have to go to the fort this time, so I did not get to see what was being done down there. We could see new buildings going up and the tents of the soldiers. The buildings are on the west side of Cache Creek or it looked so from Camp Seventh.

We could see Gen. Sheridan sitting under an awning in front of his tent. Gen. Custer has not returned from his visit to the Indian camps. Until he comes back we will not know how soon we will have to leave here.

We called the new fort, Elliott, but the War Department has not decided on the real name. We only got a day's ration for the regiment and it was issued after we returned. Unless a train arrives soon we will have to go on half rations as we are short today. Our guard duty is pretty light, for we can sit on a box and see all we have in store and it requires only one guard at a time.

The next ball game will be played next Saturday. A diamond has been made on the opposite side of Slough Creek from our camp. Some of the officers have fast horses and a race is likely to come off soon. They are over across the creek prospecting for a race track. Capt. Pliley and Lieut. McCollister have the race horses.

Tuesday, January 26, 1869

We had quite a rain last night but I did not have to be outside as we can stay under cover and guard all we have and not be very vigilant. The boys are practicing baseball in all the companies, and the officers are talking horse races. A baseball diamond is being graveled and a race track is being cleared off.

Adjt. Steele was over to our tent today and asked me when we wanted to go hunting again and I told him tomorrow.　He said all right and in a little while he came back and handed me a pass for two.

Vann has to be on duty tomorrow so Gus Ingleman and I will go.　It has cleared off and good prospects for good hunting.

Wednesday, January 27, 1869

It is warm and pleasant so we got an early start for the mountains.　We travel nearly all the forenoon and see nothing to shoot.　The game has either been killed or has been scared out of the hills.　I came upon a dead animal that had been killed by somebody quite recently that we concluded must be a mountain lion for it very much resembled the lioness in the animal shows in the East.　It was larger than any dog I ever saw and looked savage.　It was nearly six feet long.　I would not like to meet a live one like it while alone in these mountains.

Thursday, January 28, 1869

We had quite a thunder shower today and the weather is cooler.　The boys have come from the company to see what success we had yesterday.　When we told them we had no success they were disappointed.　When I went to see Adj. Steele he said there would be no more passes as small bands of Indians are in this part of the country.　They have been seen by our pickets and some have been at the fort to see what was being done there.　The scouts sent out have met some of the Indians and they do not seem to like having us so near to stay.

Now that we cannot go outside we will have to do something in camp to get us some excitement.　The boys are bringing in centipedes, horned toads and tarantulas, and trying to get up a scrap with them.

Friday, January 29, 1869

Our company and Company E are practicing for the big game tomorrow. It is quite cold today and we go over to the company and stand around the fires and the boys want to know all about our hunting trip and any news we have heard as to our next move or how soon we are likely to start home. The officers are training their race horses this afternoon on the new track they have cleared off.

Saturday, January 30, 1869

It is a nice and warm day again and hardly seems like winter as there has been no snow for about a month. Some of the boys have very fancy sweetbrier pipes they have made from the roots of the briers farther down the creek. They make them with pocket knives and several are very good specimens of hand carving. They are going to keep them to take home with them. They have no tobacco to smoke now.

The baseball game was almost a fizzle as the balls were soon knocked to pieces and they had only two, but when the game was called off Company E had 3 runs to L's 2 and L's time to go to the bat. I think this will probably end the ball games, and horse racing is all the talk. I do not know yet when the first race will come off.

The mail came in today and I received a letter from my uncle, Lewis Spotts, living at Lee's Summit, Missouri. I have never seen him or his family, but he has invited me to come and see them as soon as I get out of service. I have not had any mail for so long that I must have a lot of it in Springhill, and I have not notified the Corbetts to forward it to me, so will get it all when I get back there. Others get mail and it makes me feel as though I were an outcast. I have written very few letters and cannot expect very many out here.

Sunday, January 31, 1869

The race track is the center of attraction just now and some of the boys are over there at work getting it levelled off. It requires the pick and shovel to smooth the high and rough places and fill up the holes.

We do not have much trouble about our horses now for the pasture is very good, and one can go and change them in a little while. We bring them in at night and feed them some corn whenever we have any. We had a couple of visitors this P. M. Two Indians came from toward the fort and rode up to the colonel's tent and said "How!" but no one could talk, so after a while they rode back again.

Monday, February 1, 1869

It has rained all night, enough to settle the fresh dirt on the new race track. Not much to amuse in camp days like this. There are no cards for they have been worn out long ago. There are a few checker games with home-made checkers. No papers to read, so all we can do is to talk about our condition or about going home in the near future. There are a few worn-out horseshoes, but the far-rier won't let us use them. Most of our horses are bare-foot, but that is all the better where the ground is soft. One company tried to start a ball game but no one was interested. It will be several days yet before they can have a race on our new track, which has been about completed. It is a mile long and ten feet wide. The first race is between Capt. Pliley's and Lieut. McCollister's horses. Some of the boys have timed them when practicing and they are very evenly matched. The boys have no money or there would be some betting. I heard that the owners of the horses have bet $100 on their horses and some of the boys have bet small amounts, payable when we have a payday before we get mustered out. Everybody seems to be in favor of one of the horses and hope their favorite will be the winner. My choice is Capt. Pliley's pony, Blossom.

Tuesday, February 2, 1869

It rained all night again last night and the wind is blowing a gale and very cold which, with the mud and everything wet, makes it very disagreeable although we have a big fire. We are now thinking of making another dugout with a fireplace so we can have shelter from the storm. We go to the creek and build a fire below the bank which shelters from the wind for we have to carry wood some distance for the fire. If we had a bridge across the creek we could get plenty of fuel much closer. The water is too cold to wade it.

Some of the men want to move camp so they will not have to take the horses so far. There are only about half the men in each company that have horses as many were taken to Fort Arbuckle to recruit. I would hate to have to give mine up as I have tried so hard to keep him in condition so I could ride when the necessity arises. I have walked half the distance we have traveled and pulled grass many days, so he would have something at night. Some of the men did not seem to care whether their horses had anything at all to eat, but were growling because they did not get enough. Perhaps they got all they deserved. Many were made to go back and curry their horses better.

Wednesday, February 3, 1869

It is still cold and windy and we lie in bed until late. Did not get up for breakfast but waited for the wind to stop blowing. We would dig a dugout but may have to move to another place soon. We have had such nice

weather that it was pleasant outside so we did not need it.
And now we are afraid to make one because we might have
to abandon it and have our work for nothing. I can see very
few people outside in the regiment so they are in bed as
there are very few fires.

Thursday, February 4, 1869

The weather has moderated considerable this morning. We have inspection of our horses today and also of
equipment which is the first time and there must be a cause
for it. It looks to me as if we may have to turn over our
horses to the Regulars, as many of them have no mounts,
or able-bodied horses. They will take the poor ones to Arbuckle to recruit. I am very much afraid I will have to
lose "Billie" for we have been close friends for sometime.
What hurts me most is that I will get no benefit for the
loss of my horse and I will have to walk all the time like the
rest of them. When I walked and led my horse he carried
part of the load, blankets, overcoat, and now I will have
to walk and carry everything.

Friday, February 5, 1869

We heard today that Gen. Custer has returned and his
mission was a success for the Indians have promised to
come in as soon as their ponies are able to travel. We may
expect them as soon as there are supplies at the new fort,
but we are likely to stay until they come in. They will not
all come at one time as only a few of the work ponies are
able to make the trip. The ponies that do the moving have
to be broken to work to the dragpoles. We had to turn our
horses and equipment to the 7th Cavalry this afternoon.
The poor ones go to Arbuckle as will those of the Seventh
which our best ones will replace. While I hated to see

mine go I have nothing to worry about and no horse to feed and groom. We have very little guard duty now, and I already begin to feel lazy.

Saturday, February 6, 1869

It is more like springtime today. Thirty of our regiment have been detailed to take condemned horses to Fort Arbuckle. They go with the wagon trains from the fort and will return with them. Horses that will lead when tied to the wagons will go that way, but some will have to be ridden or led on foot. I go with some of the company boys to the top of the hill and we roll a few rocks down the side. Some go a long distance without striking anything, some go into the creek with a splash. We soon got tired as it was hard work.

The great race came off this afternoon and Capt. Pliley's pony won, but it was a close race. Lieut. McCollister and his friends are not satisfied and have challenged Capt. Pliley for another trial soon, to which he has agreed. There are other races on and one is a "slow race" which means *slow* and the horses have to keep moving all the time and not stop or the other is winner. Then there have been a few challenges for foot races so we are in for a race "craze" —a sack race, one-leg race, blind race to find the goal post and any other kind they can invent.

Sunday, February 7, 1869

It is disagreeable again today and we have a shower occasionally. The rain is mixed with snow. I am on duty every third night and none at all during the day. I have been over with the company all the afternoon. Capt. Finch wanted me to do some work on the books, crediting the boys with horses and equipment they turned in. I asked him if he wanted me to be returned to the company and he said for me to stay where I was for I had a better time than if I was there. He said, "When you have a good thing stay with it."

We have two cooks now, only one mess. The cooking is the hardest job we have and our cook said he wanted an assistant, so John Martin and Frank Van Horn are the cooks and we relieve them from guard duty when they are chosen. Duncan McCarty is sick today so some of us will have to go in his place tonight. I would rather go on guard duty than cook for I tried it once and tried to cook a gallon of rice in a two-gallon kettle and soon had everything full of rice and had to take it off the fire before it was done. We all had rice for several meals.

Monday, February 8, 1869

It began to rain in the night and is still raining this morning, but soon began to break away and before noon was clear. There is a lot of mud in camp and the creek has risen considerable, making quite a noise. We have enough to eat but would like to go hunting and have a change, but think there is very little chance to get a pass. The Indians are coming in for they can be seen by our pickets every day and their camp is across the creek and above the new fort. We are to stay here until they all come in and then the 10th Infantry will occupy the new fort and we will go home or somewhere else.

Tuesday, February 9, 1869

Three private horses were stolen last night, and one of them was Capt. Pliley's pony, Blossom. None of our men are missing, but three are gone from other companies and come in later. It may be that the horses have gotten loose and may be found. Some think they have been stolen and hidden for a few days when the men will disappear. Capts. Finch and Pliley are out looking for a trail and have found tracks of loose horses, wandering around outside the camp, but saw nothing of them. It may be that the Indians have gotten inside our pickets and stolen them. Whoever stole them had a friend in the camp guard for the horses could not have gotten outside the camp without some one knowing it. The pickets are farther apart and they might possibly get by them in the dark.

Wednesday, February 10, 1869

The horses stolen two nights back were those of Capt. Pliley, Capt. Payne of Company H and Lieut. Thresher, regimental quartermaster. Capts. Pliley and Finch are still out looking for them. They must have found a trail or they would be back. There are three men missing this morning again and are the same as yesterday, so they are likely to be gone for good this time. One of the men missing is from Company H. It is he probably who took Capt. Payne's horse. If on the trail, the officers are both good scouts and are more than equal to the three they are after, who may not be expecting to be followed, for deserters have not been followed heretofore. Capt. Pliley has a good field glass and can see them for miles. He intended to go down to the Seventh's camp and get one of Gen. Custer's best Osage Indian trailers to help hunt their trail. We may see them coming in with the three horse thieves in a few days and no telling what the penalty will be.

The soil in our camp is so soft and mellow that it soon becomes muddy. It is much worse than it has been at any time. The boys want to move somewhere else, and get out of the mud.

Thursday, February 11, 1869

It has gotten so muddy around headquarters that they could stand it no longer, so we have orders to move today.

We are camping farther up and across the creek. The creek is back of us now, and the tents face the south and the regimental headquarters to the west, toward the mountains. Our camp with the commissary is also west of Company A, with L and E companies south of A. Our squad is camped on the creek and north of the parade ground. It is a very beautiful place and near water.

We went out with a team and got a load of good wood, so we can have a big bonfire tonight and we can expect all the clerks and orderlies from headquarters to enjoy our good fire. There are lots of pine trees along the hillside close to our camp on the left and east.

We are now close to the race track, but there will be no more horse races until Capt. Pliley returns with his Blossom, which he will use every effort to recapture. Lieut. McCollister has no one who will race with him for they know they have no horses which can beat his pony.

We have been all day moving and getting our tents up and getting wood. We heard that Gen. Custer had visited the Arapahoes and Comanches and then went to see Little Robe of the Cheyennes and had a hard time getting him to agree to come in. They would not go south, but promised to go to Camp Supply early in the spring. There was a portion of the band under another chief named Medicine Arrow who, Little Robe said, was controlled by two chiefs, Big Head and Dull Knife, who were outlaws from their tribe and who had committed all the murders of settlers and other crimes which had been laid on the Cheyennes for which all had to suffer.

LITTLE ROBE, CHEYENNE WAR CHIEF FOLLOWING
THE DEATH OF BLACK KETTLE

—From the Collection of E. A. Brininstool.

Friday, February 12, 1869

This is a beautiful day and the boys over in the companies are laying off the parade ground with a parking space in front of their tents and outside the walks so as to resemble the streets in a city. They are planting the parking spaces with flowers and bringing pine trees from the hillside and planting them several feet deep. They have just cut them off and planted them but they look like real ornamental trees. They are planting them all around the parade ground and make a wonderful improvement. We got a large tree that took a dozen men to drag it down to camp and have planted it in front of the big tent. None of the trees have roots and look just as well without. The officers take as much interest as anybody and are thinking of having trees planted around their quarters, but the boys have taken all the smaller ones and those remaining are six inches or more in diameter and too large to bring.

It has been the busiest day in camp since the day we moved over here. Tonight we have a big bonfire, with all the clerks and orderlies and our company. I had quite a visit with Lieut. Col. Moore's orderly who told me what his duties were. They all had a big mess tent where they ate their meals and his first duty was to make a fire in Col. Moore's tent, then feed and curry his horse. After breakfast he cleaned up the tent, made the bed, shined boots and then he had to take the horse to graze for two hours. After that he had an hour to himself. He had to do the washing of clothing and bedding, shine buckles, scabbards and sabers. Sometimes the colonel would help him do some of his work. He was not an enlisted man and was paid $40 per month. He said all the officers' orderlies had about the same to do.

Saturday, February 13, 1869

It was quite windy this morning and some of the trees are leaning badly so the boys are out making them straight again and tamping the ground so hard they will stand all the wind pressure. The camp looks so much improved that the officers' portion of the camp is a disgrace and they are going to take the wagons and bring in large trees of the same size. We are now digging a dugout for our tent which we know how to appreciate.

There are a good many Indians coming in lately and some of them have made us a visit. They do not get off their ponies, but come up to some of the boys and just say "How!" and if you talk to them they grunt and go on. They pretend they do not understand. None of them have guns, but each one has a revolver and some of them have two. They have as good saddles as we have, and their bridles are made from buckskin braided in fancy colors and ornamental. They wear buckskin clothing and a blanket, with nothing on their heads unless on the warpath when they wear their war bonnets, decorated with beads and feathers.

Sunday, February 14, 1869

There is a grand review of the regiment today and we have to turn out with our companies. Col. Crawford has resigned and is to bid us farewell as he is going home to see if he can get the War Department to pay us for we have not seen the color of money since we left Kansas. He may have to go to Washington, but he has our best interests at heart and will do all he can for us.

Lieut.-Col. Moore is now our colonel, and Maj. Jones is lieutenant-colonel and there are several other promotions in the regiment. We were formed in lines at one side of the parade ground facing Col. Crawford's quarters, when he came out and talked to us a few minutes and thanked us for so cheerfully sharing all the hardships the regiment has had to endure, and promised to use his best endeavors to have our pay ready by the time our term of enlistment expires. He then said he would be pleased to meet any of us personally, then bid us farewell. He has been very kind to everybody and would never leave us out here so far from civilization were he not doing us ₍a great favor, for his offering of the regiment to the Government, and we had to endure such shameful treatment.

Monday, February 15, 1869

This is a day that comes to all men with a sense of great importance. It is my 21st birthday and the day when my citizenship begins. In fact I am a man. We went down to the camp of the 7th Cavalry to witness the departure of Gen. Sheridan, Col. Crawford and Capt. Jenness of Company F of our regiment for Topeka, Kansas.

Gen. Sheridan has been with us ever since we left Camp Supply and had his headquarters with us, camping in a tent when the weather was fair or foul, marching at our head in snow and rain, enduring all the hardships of wind and weather. He is not a young man either, between 35 and 40 years old.

All our commissioned officers and many privates were there and were in line with the Regular troops to see them off for the north. After we had formed two paralleled lines Gen. Custer came riding in front with Gen. Sheridan, followed by Col. Crawford and Col. Cook of the Seventh. These were followed by several cavalry officers, among them Capt. Jenness. After arriving at the top of the hill Gen. Custer and two others returned and the departure had taken place. We had some compliments from the Seventh for the manner in which our line was formed and our conduct while in line, but we only did what they did as near as we could and in that way we had to be shown.

This is the first time the two regiments have been in line together and we could see what good training does for troops. We surely were awkward in all our movements although they said we did pretty well. The day was beautiful and most of us wished we could have gone along although we have a beautiful camp and having worked hard to make it so, we should stay a while and enjoy it.

Tuesday, February 16, 1869

While we are dismounted cavalry we have to drill as infantry. I suppose it is done to keep us occupied and that we may learn more the duties of a soldier. Lieut. Johnston is acting as major now and our squad has to turn out and drill with our companies. Some of the boys would much rather put in the time marching north.

We have been out here four months now and have no more prospect of having a scrap with the Indians than we had the first month. The Indians, camped across the creek, are as well or better armed than we, for they have guns, revolvers, bows and arrows and some carry tomahawks. They have pretty good ponies, so when they come out where we can view them they put on quite a warlike appearance. We want to go over and visit their camp to see how they appear at home. We continue our camp duties. One man on duty in the daytime and two during the night.

Wednesday, February 17, 1869

Capt. Finch and Capt. Pliley returned last night with the stolen horses, but did not bring back the horse thieves. They were deserters from our regiment and had taken the horses and hid them and came back to camp again, but left for good the next night. They had ridden the horses around camp inside the camp guard so the officers would think the horses had gotten loose and were still wandering away. Capt. Pliley had gotten Custer's Indian trailers to hunt the trail. They made a circuit of several miles and discovered the trail going south toward Red River. Then the Indians returned and the officers followed the trail, which was plain as the ground was soft. The fourth day they discovered the thieves through Capt. Pliley's field glass and located the camp in the night by the fire they had built.

Early in the morning they walked in on them before they had gotten up and here the officers refused to tell more. They brought back their guns, but no men. They did not say they killed them, but Capt. Pliley said "They were looking at the sun" when they last saw them. Capt. Finch said they did not kill them, so we are left to surmise what we want to. From what I know of Capt. Finch I cannot believe he would shoot any man except in self defense, neither would he show the white feather, because he is as brave as he is good. A gentleman always.

Capt. Finch related the capture at the close of our service. "We came to their camp before daylight, and when they were about to get up we walked up to their camp and told them to get up and hold up their hands. Their clothes were placed some distance away and they were marched to them and told to put them on. Then we faced them toward the rising sun and told them to march and not look back or he would take a shot at them. They obeyed our orders to the letter and that was the last we saw of them."

Thursday, February 18, 1869

We are having some nice, warm and very pleasant weather now and the hills are green and some wild flowers are in bloom. By getting on top of the hill near camp we can see the Seventh's camp two miles away and the new fort two or three miles farther down the creek.

We can see some of the Indian tepees across the creek below the Seventh's camp. Some of the boys got outside and have been over to see the Indian camp. The women and girls hardly show themselves, but the children come close and they talk to each other. One old squaw came and held out her hand and said "money" but she got nothing.

The young boys have a game played very much like horseshoes, but use arrows. They stand at one stake and pitch them with the hand toward the other stake thirty or forty feet away, and many stuck the arrows within a few inches of the stake. They also shoot at a mark with bow and arrows a distance of fifty feet or more and it is seldom they miss by more than a few inches. Some of them can shoot an arrow as true as most men can shoot a gun. No one had anything to say to the boys who went over there. They were not molested either going in or coming out of the camp. Our mail came in today and I did not get anything so I have none to answer.

Friday, February 19, 1869

We were called out today to drill and made a great show. They called it a battalion drill, and it was different from that of the cavalry. The men who were detailed to go to Fort Arbuckle returned today. They brought corn for the cavalry horses, but no grub for the men and we are running short. The Indians are getting their supplies from the fort and we may have to go there too.

There was trouble at the Seventh's camp today. Some Indians came in and were walking through the camp when one picked up an overcoat lying on a wagon tongue and put it under his blanket. The owner saw him do it, and told him to stop and put it back but he went on, when the soldier called to him the second time, but he walked on and the soldier then shot and killed him.   All the other Indians hurried out and went to their camp, but in an hour or so about twenty Indians came in on ponies and looked at the dead one and then called for the "Big Chief."   Gen. Custer had not allowed anyone to go near the dead Indian and when they came in he told them about it and he had the soldier under arrest.   They then went to the dead one and found the coat under his blanket as the man had said.   They wanted the soldier delivered to them, but did not get him.   They finally took their warrior and returned to their camp, but not satisfied.

Saturday, February 20, 1869

We have been notified to allow no one to go outside our camp, as it is not safe for a white man to go alone anywhere beyond the camp guards for fear the Indians will retaliate for the loss of one of their number.

Our squad does not have to drill any more unless we want to go.   We are issuing only half rations today.   We are out of some things, sugar, salt and soap.   We hear more complaints about tobacco than anything.   We had a horse race this afternoon and I think everyone in the regiment was there.   The race was between Capt. Pliley's Blossome and Lieut. McCollister's Star Face.   Capt. Pliley's pony won again by only a couple feet, and it was an even race most of the way.   As usual there was more or less betting on the race and I heard that the owners had $100 on their ponies.

It is estimated that there are 800 warriors in the camp across the creek.   We have had no visitors today and are not likely to see any for some time, as they do not like the treatment the soldiers give them.   They have the best of it though, for they can go anywhere hunting or on a picnic, but we have to stay inside our camps or take a chance of losing our scalps, especially if the Indian killed was a noted warrior.

Sunday, February 21, 1869

One of Company L's young privates deserted last night. He told some of the boys he had all he wanted of this outfit and he had about made up his mind to go where he could get all he could eat again. Any man takes his life risk when he starts out alone this far from civilization, and in a hostile country.

It is cold and windy today and we are glad we do not have to go on inspection. We stay in our tent and sit by the fireplace or we can lie down on our bed. A large herd of cattle has arrived at the new fort and we will be supplied with fresh meat. I suppose of course the Indians will draw beef rations too and the herd will not last long. Indians do not get bread or flour.

We are at a loss to know what our next move will be as we have nearly two months before our term of enlistment expires and all the Indians have come in and are drawing rations, except the Cheyennes, who have promised to come in, except Medicine Arrow's band. They are the ones we are anxious to meet and make them come in or treat them like Black Kettle's band was treated.

Little Robe's band is anxious to be on a reservation where they will not be punished as all will be that remain off reservations. It is to compel them to come in, that we are down here. We cannot do much as infantry for we cannot catch Indians on their ponies, so our usefulness has passed, and we can only expect to go home to be laughed at as Indian fighters who didn't fight.

Monday, February 22, 1869

It is still cold and windy and snowing a little once in a while. We can issue only ten crackers to the man per day, but they have plenty of meat. We are expecting another provision train in a couple of days. We have some chronic grumblers who say they have not had a square meal since we started, and the habit has grown on them so they would not be satisfied with fried chicken and gravy. We have very little salt, and fresh meat requires a lot of it. Our mess has some yet, and may get along until we get more. Several of the boys have gone hunting in the mountains but the game has all disappeared. No one has killed a deer or turkey for a month. We do not get over a pound of meat for a day's ration and no salt to go with it. The men are very much discontented and won't go on guard duty until they get something to eat.

It looks like we are going to have trouble, for a good many say they will not obey if they are ordered to appear for any duty. That means guard house, but there will be no guard. It has not been like this before and we do not know what will happen tomorrow. There are only two or three companies who have rebellious men in them and we may be called out to decide if we will be obedient.

Tuesday, February 23, 1869

It is quite pleasant today. I got one letter, the first for a long time. Our mail comes once a week by carrier. Much more comes in than goes out because we have neither material nor stamps and no money to buy them. There was a mutiny today in A and L companies because they were not fed better. Of course our officers cannot help it for they are as short of provisions as we. The mutineers refused to drill or go on guard, and the leaders were put under arrest. The men begin to show in their faces that they have not been fed properly and as we have no soap, they are very ragged and dirty. All are ready to go home and it seems there is nothing to keep us here now.

It has been reported that the Cheyennes are on the way, but they are 100 miles or more from here and it will take several days for the first arrivals. They have plenty of ponies, but few are broken in to their method of moving. We are kept so close to camp and have so little freedom the men become dissatisfied. Two Indians came into our camp today and they were armed with good guns, two revolvers each and bows and arrows. They rode all over camp and stopped in front of headquarters and said "How!" to the guard on duty there. That was all they had to say to anyone. Possibly they came to see how many there were of us, so they could report.

Wednesday, February 24, 1869

Several more men were put in the guard house today for mutiny. There are a number from Company A also in the guard house which is a place roped off near headquarters with a few dog tents for sleeping quarters. They get such poor fare that some are willing to obey orders already. They have a good many visitors who stand outside the guard and talk to them. Some of them want the prisoners to agree to obey orders and be released for we are soon to have better rations and they will not get their portion until they surrender. We draw one-third pound of tobacco today and while I do not use it I take it and keep it for friends who do.

Some of the boys sent to Arbuckle for some cards and they are being used to pass the time now. They are gambling for tobacco and cut it in small cubes and bet them. I can play several games, but have not learned any of the gambling games. We could bet on all the games and the winner takes the pot, but as I am not an expert at any of them, I do not feel interested enough to try to win anything. It is colder today and as our duty is light we change often so we can go to the fire and get warm.

Thursday, February 25, 1869

It has been pretty cold today and I have been on duty part of the time. They still drill in the companies; probably to keep the men from being dissatisfied. The mail came today and I got a letter from home and I was very glad to hear that all were well. It had been forwarded from Springhill. I am sorry I cannot answer it. No material nor money.

We heard the paymaster has been at the Seventh's camp but never came near us. We have no sutler and cannot hope to have one as long as we have no money to spend for his goods. I do not think a dollar could be found in our whole regiment for I think our officers are as bad off as their men, so a sutler would not do business if he were to come just now.

Gen. Custer and another officer came up to our headquarters today and called on Col. Moore. The clerk on duty there visited our fire tonight and told us that the Cheyennes were not coming in though they had agreed to do so and the cavalry may have to go after them, and we are to stay here until they return. They are not certain what the orders will be, but that is the supposition of the troops in the field, so it may be that we will have to stay here another month and perhaps longer.

Friday, February 26, 1869

It is another pleasant day and I have to do duty for George Vann, who is not very well. We have taken W. F. Sloan in our tent for they had a quarrel in their mess and he is through with them. It makes us a little crowded, but Will is a nice fellow, well liked by all of us, so we gladly take him in. Will is part Irish but was so disgusted with them he could stand it no longer. None of the squad is very much attached to them either.

Saturday, February 27, 1869

It is cloudy today, but warm and pleasant. We had another horse race this afternoon and everybody but the guards was there. The track was in pretty good condition and the race was between the same horses as the other races. This time Lieut. McCollister's pony won by a half neck and now he has won his $100 back, but I think he still owes Capt. Pliley a hundred. After the race there was a game of baseball and a foot race. The latter was won by a man in Company I. They ran one-quarter mile and the winner beat by 45 yards. The baseball game was between Companies A and E, and Company A won, 13 to 9.

Sunday, February 28, 1869

Today has been pleasant and I went over to visit the company. I saw a man sitting all alone on the company parade ground and went down to see who it was and found it was J. A. Studabecker, bucked and gagged. I spoke to him but he was unconscious, and his eyes were wide open and staring. I hurried up to Capt. Finch and told him. He had heard nothing of it, but jumped up and went over to Lieut. Stoddard's tent and asked him if he did it. He said he did it to punish the man for stealing part of a ham from Capt. Pliley's tent during the night. When told he was about dead we hurried and took the gag out of his mouth and unloosed him so he could breathe, but it took some vigorous rubbing to bring him to. Then I never heard a man talked to as Capt. Finch talked to Lieut. Stoddard. He

told him he had a mind to call a guard and have him put in
the same fix.   He also said there were plenty of men in the
company who would delight to do it.   Lieut. Stoddard
heard it all and then went to his tent.   Later Studabecker
told his story as follows: Last night about 10:30 a man
came to him while he was preparing as cook for breakfast
and asked for a knife a few minutes.   He gave him his
butcher knife and pretty soon he returned the knife and a
piece of ham with it, and went away.

Monday, March 1, 1869

We drew beef, salt, soap and tobacco and now the boys
are happy.   We can clean up our faces and clothes and look
respectable again.   Went over to the company again today
and had quite a talk with J. A. Studabecker when he told
me that he could not help having a piece of ham.   The fellow was a stranger and went away, so he hardly got a good
look at him, and when the guard came and searched the
tents he made no effort to conceal the ham and gave them
as good a description of the fellow as he could.   He told me
he would never forget me for had I not come to his relief
when I did he soon would have been dead.

Lieut. Stoddard and Lieut. Brady of Company E are
both from New York   and   good   friends.   Today   Lieut.
Brady showed his authority by making a spread-eagle of a
man to punish him.   He made the man lie on his back,
spread out his arms and legs, then drove a stake at each
hand and one at each foot and tied his hands and feet to
the stakes.   Capt. Payne of Company H came up the line
and saw him lying there.   He went to Capt. Finch and they
called Capt. Pliley.   Together they went over to Company
E and asked Capt. Darling why that man was in that condition.   Capt. Darling said he did not know anything about
it.   He called Lieut. Brady and Brady said, "Yes, I did it,

and would do it again if the party was guilty of the same offense."

Payne replied, "I hear you are a West Pointer and we came over here to tell you that punishment of that kind might be the law at West Point, but we have a different idea of punishment of that kind on the frontier. I've brought witnesses to what I will do to you if you do not immediately untie that man."

Brady did not move very quickly and big Capt. Payne just laid his big hand on him and said, "Loose him!" and he did so with trembling fingers, but he got the cords loose. All those of our company who witnessed it wished that Lieut. Stoddard had come over and had seen Capt. Payne and heard the lecture he gave Lieut. Brady.

It has been decided to call the new fort, Fort Sill. It is about completed and the 10th Cavalry (colored) will remain in charge of the fort at present. The Seventh will escort us as far as Camp Supply where the Cheyennes are to come in on a reservation near the camp. The orders are for us to proceed to Fort Hays, Kansas, and there be mustered out.

Tuesday, March 2, 1869

Everybody is happy this morning because we are preparing to leave for home. About 8 o'clock a train came up from the Seventh's camp and we loaded all the tents and cooking kits. Some of the boys have a lot of keepsakes they have picked up on our trip, but they are not allowed to take anything except those things necessary for the trip, unless they want to carry them. Some have put their overcoats in the roll with their bedding and in that way they do not have to carry them. Had we been going any place but home we would leave here in sorrow, for it is the most homelike camp we have had.

It is nearly noon before the 7th Cavalry arrive and we fall in behind and march up Slough Creek toward the mountains almost west from our old home for months past. On looking back we could see the rows of pines we had planted, and the hill behind it, covered with green grass and pine trees, but we never expected to visit it again.

The land on Cache and Slough Creeks is very rich, and there are wild sunflowers a couple of inches thick a few inches from the ground and ten to fifteen feet high. How I would like to own a quarter section in this creek bottom!

The mountains across the creek are high and the stream is not so wide but runs more swiftly for we are going up hill all the time. We do not see any pine trees here, but there are a good many on the mountain side, some of them quite large, for some distance from the creek and oak trees and some underbrush.

We go into camp about an hour before dark after going four or five miles. It is not far from where George Vann and I killed the deer and turkeys. The deer were near the underbrush and the turkeys roosted in the oaks. We did not see any game this evening except a few quail and one little rabbit.

Wednesday, March 3, 1869

We started about 7 o'clock this morning with the 7th Cavalry in the lead, our regiment following, all on foot, except the officers. We have returned to our companies and Billie Mather says for us to stay with the "grub wagon" and he would see that we got our regular rations, so we walk with the wagon train, Vann and I in the lead so we are just behind our regiment. Company K is the last company and I have a chance to talk with Orlando Soward of that company whom I knew in Indiana when we were boys about 12 years old.

We are still on the south side of the creek as there are no streams flowing into it from that side for the valley is to our left but not so level. We carry only our guns for we have packed our overcoats in our bedding to which no objection was made. We can easily march as fast as the wagons and have nothing to do for we are guarding the wagons as we are walking and can see the train all the time.

We have no sergeant as he has been with his company for some time. We take our orders from Sergt. Mather and he lets us do whatever we please when off duty, which is very nice of him.

Occasionally we see the officer of the day who is one of the 7th Cavalry. He came along this afternoon and asked where we belonged and Vann told him we were train guards and he said no more to us. Once in a while we come across some one who has stopped and let his company go on, hoping to get a ride in a wagon but we are there to see that he keeps out of our portion of the train.

Thursday, March 4, 1869

It has been very disagreeable today, wind blowing pretty hard and raining at times. For a while it was nearly frozen rain which made us wish for overcoats. We will keep our coats outside hereafter or put them in a wagon where we can get them when needed. Our course is now nearly west and we have left the creek and the road is quite rough in places so the pioneer corps has to work hard and fast so we can make better time. After going about 20 miles we camp about 4 o'clock in a place where there had been a camp a long time ago. We can see the holes where they had dugouts. The scouts say it was the camping place of the 3rd Dragoons on their way to Mexico during the Mexi-

can War. There are dead logs that have been cut with an
ax. We are leaving the mountains behind since 2 or 3
o'clock.

Friday, March 5, 1869

The storm is over and nearly clear again. The sun
shines warm and pleasant. We have very little trouble
crossing ravines as we seem to be following an old road
which is pretty good except for washouts. We are still
traveling west and we want to go north.

Vann and I were some distance ahead of the train about
4 o'clock when we passed two soldiers lying on a mound on
our left. When we were the nearest to them someone fired
a gun and the ball passed so close to our faces that we
imagined we could feel the air from it. Just then one of
the men jumped to his feet and grabbed his comrade. We
stopped and he said, "Come here, quick!" When we came
close we saw that the man had been shot and I hurried
toward the train for help and met the trainmaster and told
him. He rode back a short distance and soon had an ambulance and we put him in it. The man shot was William
Gruber, our chief bugler, who appeared to me to be dead.
He was shot in the head. We could see some boys on the
right who were apparently shooting at prairie dogs.

We came on to a camp that the 7th Cavalry had located
for the wagon trains, near North Fork of Red River. There
was considerable excitement in camp over the accident for
Gruber was generally a favorite with everybody. After
we had our supper we went to see what the fuss was about
for officers were hurrying in all directions and soon learned
that the man who fired the fatal shot was Wm. J. Froman
of Company L, and he was under arrest for the shooting.
A Court of Inquiry was held and after witnesses were ex-

amined it was decided it was an accident from not being careful about the direction he was shooting.

The company buglers were called together and asked to select a chief bugler from their number. Two men were put in nomination, Enoch Collett of Company F and Rolla R. Watt of Company L. The vote stood five for Collett and four for Watt. Both men were good men and good buglers, but Collett was the senior.

The scouts have reported an Indian trail a few miles from the river on the west side. Gen. Custer is very anxious to follow it for it may be a portion of the Cheyennes and he wants to give them an idea of his power to compel them to go on a reservation. A consultation is being held between the officers of both regiments, so we may have to go home alone from here with perhaps a scout or two to lead us. We have marched twenty-eight miles today. I have not been to the company all day, but go to bed early. There is a commotion in some of the wagon trains and considerable loud talking among the teamsters.

Saturday, March 6, 1869

Reveille at 4 o'clock and breakfast before daylight. Our chief bugler was buried, with the honors of war, before the sun came up.

There is quite an excitement over in the companies and I go to see what it is all about. One of the boys told me that Gen. Custer had called on our regiment for volunteers to go with the Seventh to follow the trail discovered yesterday by the scouts and that Capt. Finch was taking the volunteers while Lieut. Stoddard was taking the balance to the Washita to wait there until the campaign was ended and the troops returned to meet them. When I learned that Capt. Finch was going I made up my mind quickly to go as a volunteer. I went to see Billie Mather and he said for me to get half of a squad to go with me and he would see that we were treated fair if we would take orders from him.

I got four others of the squad to go, but our train had been gone half an hour when we started and the rear guard was about to start when we got in line "four abreast" and started after our train. We followed as fast as we could and once in a while we could see our train in advance and also the rear guard who started shortly after we did.

We did not catch up to our portion of the train until nearly noon, and did not see Mather until after we went into camp. We had packed our blankets and overcoats besides our guns and were glad to get part of our load in the commissary wagon. After we had gone about twenty-five miles we halted and the orders came for everybody to make coffee and eat lunch for we would march again in an hour toward a fire which could be seen in the west and supposed to be started by Indians.

Company L was quite near the wagons and I asked Capt. Finch if I had not better go back to the company. He asked me if I had any rations and I told him what Sergt. Mather told me. He said I had better stay with Mather until ordered to my company. After talking with some of the boys I was about to go back when I saw a couple of sergeants taking Orderly Sergt. Ike S. Elder and placing him under guard. Asking what he had done, I was told, "Disobedience to orders."

We are now with the wagons and probably will be during this campaign. I could not think of staying behind for I could not trust Lieut. Stoddard and he might have sent me to my company again. When I was over at the company they were drawing rations and I was given my share and Vann had gotten my portion from Mather, so I had plenty. We are going to eat sparingly for we are told that it may be a week before we return to the place where a train is to meet us.

We wait until it begins to get dark before we start out for the fire. We march until nearly midnight before we come to the burning grass, but see no signs of Indians. We find a patch of several acres where the grass is not burned because it is too green or wet. We camp in this spot, but there is not wood or water, so we go to bed, but the mules keep braying so we can't sleep much. Mules seem to take that method to let the teamsters know they are thirsty. We hope to find water early in the morning so we can make coffee. We have come at least forty miles today and that is more than the men can stand for any length of time.

Sunday, March 7, 1869

We do not hear any bugles this morning, but the men are up at 4, and everybody is ready to march at daylight. We are going up the Salt Fork of Red River and sometimes we are quite close to the stream. The water is too salty to drink and in places we can see crusts of salt like ice at the edge of the water. Some of us break off these crusts of salt and fill our pockets for we may be in need of salt as we have often been before on our march.

We are certainly having a great time as we have no duty to do, go wherever we please and as fast as we please so we do not come in contact with the officer of the day or rear guard. We are on the Indian trail, but it is a small band of not more than a dozen for they build only one fire, but there are quite a number of pony trails. The day has been fine.

Monday, March 8, 1869

It began to rain early this morning and we have to wear our overcoats which began to get quite heavy after they got wet. We have been following the trail all day and passed two of the Indians' camping places, so they have not been traveling very fast. At the last camp they left some fire, so they must be pretty close to us. Early this afternoon the scouts came back and reported an Indian camp in advance. It was raining pretty hard, but we had been carrying our guns under our coats, so the water could not get in the magazines and wet the cartridges. We were told to halt while the cavalry made the attack. We stood in the rain until the "battle" was over and then were ordered to advance and go into camp near that of the Indians. It was then we heard about the attack. There were eight Indians and one squaw in the party. The Indians had probably not returned from the hunt and the squaw had the meal on the fire when the Seventh came in sight. She left everything, jumped on a pony and started for the left side of a circular piece of small timber to the right. Gen. Custer took the other side of the timber, expecting to head her off, but she never came that way, but went up a small ravine to her left and up on the plains. By the time her trail was found she was out of sight and miles away for they saw her no more.

The "battle" resulted in no casualties and no captures except two tents, eleven ponies, some blankets and some buffalo meat they were to have for their evening meal. The camp was a curiosity and nearly everyone went to see it. No one wanted what they left, not even the ponies, except two that were exchanged for horses by the Seventh, and the others were killed. The other plunder was burned. We are having a joke on the Seventh for letting the Indians escape.

This is probably the end of our trip for we have no more trail to follow and we have very little more than enough provisions to last until we get back to the Washita, where we are to meet a train.

Tuesday, March 9, 1869

All the officers of both regiments and the chief of scouts held a council last night to determine what was best to do now. Our provisions are nearly all gone and would not any more than last until we got back to the Washita where more will be waiting for us. Many of the officers felt that it was best to go ahead for a few days as we were now in the Indian country and the Cheyennes could not be more than a couple of days march from us, but we did not know just where to find them.

Nearly all expressed themselves, that while it might seem inadvisable to proceed in our condition, they had an intuition that victory was near, or that we were being led by some unseen power, for the accomplishment of some good purpose, and it was finally decided to push on for three or four days and see what the result would be. So this morning we are on the march again toward the west, but following no trail. The scouts think the Indians we have been following were on their way to their camp from a hunting trip for they had considerable meat partly cured with them. By going in the same direction we are most likely to run across their camp or some trail that would lead to it. We have been going over high level country all day and have come to no streams or timber, but have been expecting to come to some fresh water tributary of Red River. We camp in a low place where there is green grass and indications of water near the surface.

I have been with my company most of the day. In all the canteens there was not enough water to make a cup of coffee for each man in the mess. About four miles back I remembered having looked for a drink, in a small pool in a deep washout, where there had been a waterfall. I thought I could easily find the place and I was very thirsty.

I took five or six canteens and started back on the trail to find that pool.

It was pretty light, but no moon, so I could see the trail easily. After getting to the place where I expected to find water, I climbed down and began my search for it, but could find none. Going back to the place where I got down I started to climb out and getting my head above the bank I saw a man on horseback following our trail. When he came quite near he stopped but I could not tell if it was an Indian or a scout. After waiting a while, and he still stood there I slipped down the ravine for a couple of hundred yards and started across country for camp, which I could easily locate by the firelight. I had no arms and so did not even wait to see if the horseman was red or white, friend or foe. When I arrived at camp the teamsters had dug a well and found water at ten feet. It was near midnight when I got in, but we had to wait until 2 o'clock to get a drink. I never had wanted a drink of water so bad in my life. While I had not had a bite to eat since breakfast I did not feel hungry while so thirsty. We finally had a cup of good coffee and ate a little and went to bed hoping we would not be called at 4 o'clock as usual. They were giving the mules and horses water all night, but we did not hear any of the noise.

Wednesday, March 10, 1869

We had to get up at 4 and got to sleep but little. We slept as long as we could and then were going to make some hot coffee before starting, but on going to the well for water we discovered that a mule had fallen in, so we had to start without coffee or breakfast and no water in our canteens. We had gone only a few miles when the command halted and were watering horses and mules when we came up. A large sulphur spring had been discovered from which flowed a nice stream, but many horses and mules as well as men did not relish the flavor and went on as thirsty as before. I had lived several years where we used sulphur water, so I did not dislike it and filled my canteen with it.

We are with the wagons today although there is nothing to eat in them except a few boxes of crackers, a little bacon and three sacks of beans. We have decided to keep together and remain with the wagons for we will fare better under Sergt. Mather here than if we go to our companies and share with the men. We can be independent except when Sergt. Mather calls on us for any kind of service and he has very little to do himself. Our squad consists of A. P. Ingleman, George Vann, Frank Van Horn, Stephen Van Dorn or the three Vans and myself. We have marched eighteen miles and camp on a fork of Red River the scouts call Gypsum Creek, very tired and sleepy.

We are pretty well acquainted with the teamsters of the provision wagons and they tell us we may sleep under the wagons. We turn in as soon as we have eaten and expect to get a good rest in sleep.

Thursday, March 11, 1869

We are up and ready to start at daylight and going southward. We have not seen any trail old or fresh since we left Salt Creek and are going farther from supplies all the time. About noon we come to a nice stream of fresh water, and we are told it is Mulberry Creek. There is plenty of good water and considerable timber so we think we have a real camp again, but after halting an hour we have orders to march again. By 3 o'clock we have come in sight of the main Red River which we can see is a wide stream with several small streams flowing among the sand bars of a river bed of over a mile wide. There is considerable timber on the south side but very little on the north side.

We have discovered a small Indian trail which, the scouts say, is about a month old. We follow it the rest of the day going northwest instead of southwest and camp on Mulberry Creek where the Indians had made their campfire. It was a small party as they had made only one fire. We went on top of a hill near our camp and can still see the main Red River.

Friday, March 12, 1869

There are several Osage Indian scouts in the command who keep ahead several miles to discover any trails and pick out the best route. These scouts are under the command of their chief, Hard Rope. Our officers held another consultation last night to determine what was best, as we have come away from our base of supplies several days' march. It is nearer to Fort Sill than any other base, but by going there we would have 150 miles or more extra to travel than by going back the way we came.

The scouts had followed the old trail some distance and it had a northeast course. To follow it we would be going almost toward the Washita camp. We cross the creek as soon as we can see and our course is almost due north which is more cheering for it is more like going home. We do not have very much to eat, but going in the right direction is a great incentive to good feeling, and we hear expressions of satisfaction quite often. Even the teamsters are delighted. If we could see a few Indians now to get up some excitement everybody would be pleased.

As we have no load and the wagons are almost empty the teamsters let a couple of us ride when the wagon master is not in sight. We carry only our guns; everything else is put in wagons. We had to stop some time today to get the wagons across a steep ravine. We were walking some distance behind the wagons this afternoon and the officer of the day came along and said, "What are you fellows doing back here?"

Vann said, "We were detailed as a commissary guard over the wagons."

"All right," the officer answered, "get up with the wagons and stay there."

We did so, as fast as we could walk. We often wonder why we are allowed to run loose like this, but as long as we can be independent of any and everybody we will go it alone. Why should we worry? We have gone twenty miles and camp on Sand Creek, a tributary of North Fork. There is much driftwood but no trees and only a small stream of water. It has been a very nice day.

Saturday, March 13, 1869

The scouts report a large Indian trail a few miles up Sand Creek, not very old and much larger than the one we have been following. We cross the creek this morning and go up the north side until we come to the trail which leads to the north. As the train is not moving very fast I conclude to hurry ahead and see how many wagons there are in the train. I had gotten pretty well toward the front and was watching the forage wagons cross a small stream, when a teamster riding the saddle mule of his team was passing. I noticed his face which seemed very familiar and he had a scar on his face I had seen somewhere in the long ago. After he had passed I hurried and passed him again, and then waited until he came up, so I could see if I could recognize him. Just as he was about to pass me, the teamster ahead called him "Simon"; then I remembered who it was. Back in Indiana my aunt lived next door and when her married daughter died she left a son about 8 years old who came and lived with his grandmother until his father married again. We had been playmates for several years, when he went to live with his father in Missouri. Then he was ten years old and I had not seen him since. I came beside his mule and asked him if he was not Simon Onstott. When he said he was I told him it was long since I had seen him, that I did not know him at first. He looked very much surprised and asked who I was. He got off his mule and took a look at me and then said, "You are Dave Spotts and look quite natural, only older."

We were together all day talking over our boyhood days, much of which we had never forgotten. After I had my supper I went to look for him. After quite a search I found him and we spent a very pleasant evening together.

We have a dry camp tonight and the mules are making the night hideous with their continuous braying. Whenever a mule or horse is too weak to travel he is left behind and before the rear guard leaves camp they are killed and any other property is burned. Wagons, saddles or harness are put in the fire so that there will be nothing the Indians can make use of.

Sunday, March 14, 1869

The night was quite cold and the ground is covered with a white frost. We have orders this morning for every man to take only one blanket besides overcoat and rations as there was going to be a sacrifice of all tents, blankets and clothing not actually necessary and all would be burned.

All the wagons were loaded very lightly and quite a number of mules were abandoned as condemned and were shot. Eight or ten wagons and a lot of harness were burned.

I picked up a good looking horse and saddle that had been left behind by the cavalry. It was too cold to ride, so

I led him and he did pretty well, then I got on him for a while until I got cold and got off again.   He did not travel as fast as the wagons and before night the wagons had passed me and the rear guard was in sight, so I had to let him go and hurry on.   It was not long until I heard a shot when I knew the horse was dead.   Then I had to hurry to catch the wagons, but before I caught up with them they had crossed a wide stream where the water was quite deep and cold, but I had to wade it.   The water was two feet deep in many places and I did not know when I would find a deep place and go under, but finally I reached the farther side, nearly frozen.   The wagons were camping and I finally located my squad who had a fire started and I greatly appreciated it just then.

We then find we have nothing at all to eat, and while I am getting warm the other boys are picking up corn that the mules have spilled out of their nose bags.   They have about a quart which we roast in our frying pan and one of the teamsters loaned us a coffee mill so we could grind it.

It is getting so cold that we are devising a plan so we can sleep and be protected from the cold.   Vann told us to go and find all the grass or leaves we could find and he would borrow a shovel and dig a hole 5 x 6 feet, a foot or more deep and fill it with grass and then we could have our blankets for covering, and also sleep in most of our clothing. Billy Mather came around hunting for us and told us we could have some fresh meat, so we drew three pounds each and have corn and meat for supper.   We are told that no more meat will be issued for three days and perhaps nothing else, but he will let us know if there will be another issue.

The teamsters seem to have plenty to eat all the time. Each one has a big mess box which is well filled when he starts out, and if he has to abandon his wagon some other teamster takes him and his mess box in his wagon. We help the teamsters to take care of their stock, help them hitch up and unhitch for we have nothing else to do. Once in a while they add a little to our fare which we appreciate and try to repay. I saw my horse, or the one I turned over, but he did not look so well. I did not get close enough to speak to his rider.

This is a freezing cold night and had we not prepared for it we would have nearly frozen. There are only three of us together as two of the Vans have gone to their company tonight, so we have only three blankets and "spoon" all night—faces all one way, and when one of us wants to turn over he says "Everybody, flop" and all turn, facing the other way.

Monday, March 15, 1869

We slept considerable last night although it was freezing cold all night and ice on the river. Fresh signs of Indians can be seen as soon as we get started and the scouts say we camped near where a large camp of Indians had been quite recently, probably less than a week ago. Their trail leads to the northeast, the direction we have been traveling for the last two days. We are told that it is very probable we will have all the fighting we want in a day or two, provided we can find their camp before they see us. Our Indian scouts keep several miles in advance of the column.

The trail is a large one now, and quite plain. We have all been ordered in front of the train before starting and our squad gets right up to the regiment, but not with it, although right behind the last company.

Orders came about 2 o'clock to hurry fast as possible as there were Indians ahead. We went on a trot for about half a mile, when we were ordered to halt and await further orders. Shortly we were ordered to proceed slowly and every man was examining his gun for we were expecting an order to attack any time, although there were no Indians in sight.

About 4 o'clock we arrived at the top of a bluff overlooking a valley a mile or more wide and a creek flowing to the right. Along the creek on the side next to us was a large Indian camp of nearly 200 lodges. We could see the 7th Cavalry coming around on the farther side of the camp and we formed in line on the south side next to us so we soon had them as near surrounded as our lines would reach.

Gen. Custer and his staff were in the Indian camp which was alive with Indians all greatly excited, but they did not have their ponies. In a short time a large herd of ponies arrived from somewhere down the creek. They were followed by a lot of mounted Indians. As soon as they reached camp they were mounted and the warriors were riding in all directions. Finally every pony had a rider and some had several women and children. They were ready to leave and we received no orders to stop them. Now was our chance for a real Indian fight, but no orders came. Gen. Custer was still in their midst, and all the time they were getting ready to make a break for escape. Suddenly they all made a dash down the creek and not a gun was fired. We were not to fire until we had the order, and when they had gotten away all the Kansas men were disgusted for this was the only opportunity we had to punish the Indians who had killed so many of the Kansas settlers. Gen. Custer was then branded by some who had lost relatives or friends, as a coward and traitor to our regiment. We had them prisoners and could have kept them without firing a gun.

There must be something important taking place as the Seventh is coming in close and surrounding the camp, while we were kept waiting for an hour or more.

Then we were ordered to form a line a few hundred yards above the camp and then go into camp for the night. After we have formed our camp, the council of chiefs is still in session. Then the Seventh also go into camp, but the Indians are not allowed to leave. We hear tonight this is Medicine Arrow's camp and the Indians have refused to go on a reservation, so they are just the ones we were most pleased to find, but would have liked very much to have given them at least some punishment, which they greatly deserved. We go to sleep tonight with our guns beside us for we are likely to need them any time.

Tuesday, March 16, 1869

We get up at the usual hour and the Indian camp is still there, but no Indians in sight for they fled without taking their tents. No one is allowed to go near or disturb them. The principal chief in this camp is Medicine Arrow, but there are two other chiefs who are war chiefs and when the tribe is at peace their power is gone, so they are not in favor of going on reservations. They are younger men and the young warriors are under their influence, so Medicine Arrow's power is a civil one. He has to be governed by the sentiment of those subject under him. We hear that there were two white women in this camp until news came of our men's approach, when they were hurried outside the camp and we did not surround the camp soon enough to intercept them.

The scouts discovered a portion of the herd of ponies and reported to Gen. Custer, who went with them. They met Medicine Arrow coming from the camp with a white flag. When he told Gen. Custer there were two white women in their camp and if he attacked them the women would be killed, orders were sent to the command to surround the camp but not to fire a shot unless fired upon, and he rode into their camp under the protection of the Indian chief.

In the camp Gen. Custer met the war chiefs, Big Head and Dull Knife, and he assured them no one would be molested unless they wanted a fight. Then they were told why we were there; to have them go on a reservation peaceably as the other tribes were doing. This they agreed to do, and when told they could go, the men, women and children lost no time getting away.

A courier was sent out telling them they could come back and get their camp and everything in it. So they came and moved their tents and belongings this forenoon. The chiefs, Medicine Arrow, Big Head and Dull Knife, are being held as security for the promises they have agreed to perform. The first to be done is to bring in the white prisoners who were taken beyond the camp along the creek which is bordered with high underbrush.

Several Indians came in and wanted to give the two women in exchange for the chiefs, but were told that was not the agreement, and the three chiefs would not be given up until they were all settled at Camp Supply. Some of the boys counted the tents and there were nearly 200, and they average six to the tent, or about 1200 Indians. It is considered some strategy to capture that many hostile Indians without firing a shot. Just now all we can show for all our long walk and starvation is three Indians whom the tribe wants badly and may fight to regain.

Wednesday, March 17, 1869

We are waiting for something to be done and it may be a fight, for no white prisoners have yet arrived, but they are holding out for an exchange which has been positively refused. We have moved our camp today, down the creek toward the camp of Little Robe. We learned there was great excitement in their camp when we moved in their direction, although Gen. Custer had informed Little Robe that he was going to move toward his camp, but had no intention of coming within eight or ten miles.

After we had camped, Gen. Custer sent a messenger asking Little Robe to visit his camp. After his arrival he assured Gen. Custer he was doing all he could to have the prisoners brought in, but they were beyond his power, and if we had to fight to get them he would not have any part in the conflict, but would try to have them brought in.

We have camped the wagons between the two regiments so we are protected on both sides. The teamsters of the two trains are visiting together. I found my cousin and he told me that one of the women prisoners was a sister of one of the teamsters. On inquiry I found he was along with this expedition to see if he could find any trace of her.

We hunted among the hundred or so teamsters and finally learned his name and found him and he gave me a good account of himself and sister. He said he was a Civil War soldier; was in a New Jersey regiment with his father and brother. His name was D. A. Brewster. Both his father and brother were killed, but he went through and was discharged and then went to their home near Trenton. The mother, sister and himself then moved to Pennsylvania where his mother died. He then left his sister with friends and went to Kansas and took up a claim of 160 acres on the Solomon River. After he had built a cabin he sent for his sister to come out and keep house for him. In the fall of the year 1867 the Indians made raids on the settlers and they had information that Indians had been seen only a few miles from their claim.

The settlers hurried their families and the old men in wagons to a place of safety. After they had gotten them started the younger men went to intercept the Indians but missed them. The Indians followed the wagon train but there were not enough to capture it, so they tried to stampede the horses by shooting and yelling, and succeeded in frightening a span of fancy horses driven by a young couple who had been recently married. This team ran away and all the Indians followed to capture the team and entirely abandoned the wagon train. Miss Brewster was with these settlers but after the scare they returned to their homes, and there was no further trouble from the Indians that year.

Last year his sister had married another settler near their claim, named James S. Morgan, and just a month after their marriage Morgan had finished gathering corn on his (Brewster's) place when he saw some Indians coming toward him. He had just gotten the horses loose from the wagon when an Indian slipped through the corn and shot him through the hip, but only a flesh wound. He left his team, which ran away. He dodged around through the corn until he came to the river where he jumped in, but they did not look in the brush for him. After they had gone he crawled out and to the wagon where he was found later and taken to the hospital. The horses ran home and it is thought Mrs. Morgan took one of the horses to go and look for her husband, thinking he had a runaway, and while on her search was picked up by the Indians, as one of the horses was gone and the other at home, loose with harness on. Next day they tracked the Indians up northwest over the divide between the Solomon and Republican rivers where there had been quite a large camp, but all had gone to the west from there. Ever since his sister's capture Brewster has been at forts and with troops, trying to find some trace of her and now he has great hopes that one of the women is she.

Indian messengers are coming and going all day, but while they are holding the women we are likely to stay here and we have nothing to eat. The excitement is so great we hear very little complaint about hunger or anything else, so it is just watchful waiting.

Thursday, March 18, 1869

We move a mile up the creek again today and below where the Indian camp was located and where there is more feed for the horses and mules. We drew three-quarters of a pound of beef today which is the last beef and we have not had a hardtack for several days. We are living on excitement now and our stomachs are getting so used to being empty that they have shrunk to fit the occasion.

Indian messengers are still coming and going but we have seen no white women. They are still holding out for the exchange and Gen. Custer is very much disgusted with their continual demand, "Want to talk some more." I understand he has told them if the prisoners are not in our camp before sundown tomorrow he will hang Big Head and Dull Knife to a large overhanging tree. He took them and showed the limb and explained it so they understood just what he meant. After that he would attack any of them he could find. It is their last chance to save the lives of their chiefs and they most likely think more of them than they do of the white prisoners. We have more ammunition now than we have provisions, so we must be on the move very soon.

Friday, March 19, 1869

It is nice and pleasant this morning and everybody is quietly waiting. We have a double line of pickets out today for we do not know whether it is war or peace, and may see Indians coming over the hills in all directions to try and rescue the prisoners held by our troops. Everyone has his gun ready for use and where it can be used quickly. Everybody is watching for the coming of the captives, but we do not know from what direction they will come. They were taken northwest and up the creek, but may be brought in from some other direction.

We hear no complaints about hunger for everybody is anxious and excited, hoping to see the prisoners brought in. The Indian chiefs are sullen and occasionally mutter something to each other. Evidently they do not like to see the lariats hanging from the willow limb.

The excitement is intense after noon. We are told that rations are being issued. The officers have divided equally with the men, even to Gen. Custer, who turned his private wagon over to the men and told them to divide what it contained among themselves, for he could live without eating as long as any of them.

Between 3 and 4 o'clock some one yelled, "Hurrah they're coming!" and to the southwest, about where we came over the hill to attack the camp, we saw three or four Indians on ponies bearing a white flag, and with them were the captives. They stopped at the picket first, and sent one of their number down the hill to our camp and informed Gen. Custer the prisoners were ready to be delivered, but they wanted two of the chiefs in exchange.

They were told that there would be no exchange, but in less than an hour there would be two dead chiefs if they were not here before that time. The messenger said, "Come out and get them."

Gen. Custer said to Col. Moore, "As these are Kansas women I detail you and your officers to receive them."

Col. Moore and Majors Jones and Jenkins rode out to the post and brought them in. As they were coming, two lines were soon formed and they passed between the lines and it surely was a pitiful sight to behold.

Before going between the lines they all dismounted and the larger woman led by Col. Moore and the other by Maj. Jones passed down the lines. The larger one appeared to be 50 years old, although she was less than 25. She was stooped, pale and haggard, looking as if she had been compelled to do more than she was able. She was quite tall, with light hair that was bleached on top until it was dirty brown from exposure. Her clothes were made of three or four kinds of material, pieces of tents and blankets, all worn out and sewed together with strings.

The other was much younger looking and did not show the hard usage. She also was pale and dressed pretty much the same. The Indians did not even allow them a blanket to cover their ragged clothing. I heard that Brewster was there when they arrived at the tent and recognized the larger one as his sister and said to her, "Oh, sister, how you must suffer!" I also heard they had made several attempts to escape but were caught every time. The Indian messenger took the pony the girls came in on and escaped as rapidly as he could.

The chiefs are not so sullen now, but the ropes still hang from the limbs and some of the boys are hoping they will be hung yet.

The prisoners are Mrs. Anna Belle Morgan and Miss Sarah C. White. The latter was captured two months before Mrs. Morgan from a settler's cabin near the Republican River. Mrs. Morgan is nearly 25 years old and Miss White 19. They have been together most of the time, in a camp of the Dog Soldiers, who are composed of outlaws from their own tribe. They lived like gypsies, moving from place to place, and got their subsistence from robbing and murdering settlers and wagon trains. They were not honest with their own people and were not allowed to mix with them.

Mrs. Morgan learned from her brother that her husband was not killed, but wounded, so she may yet get to see him. Miss White does not know if her people were killed, for the last she saw of her mother she was forced inside their cabin and the girl was taken by force and bound to a pony and carried away. Both women have had a hard life to endure as their faces show. They did not even smile when they were brought in.

Saturday, March 20, 1869

Reveille at 4 and we march at 6 and think we are going home, but camp a short distance above the abandoned Indian camp. We can now see where the tents stood. Some of the boys found a dead Indian woman, covered with brush. She was very old and in their haste to leave, the Indians had not taken time to bury her. Those who found the body took shovels and piled dirt over her several feet high so the wolves will hardly find her.

We are entirely out of supplies and have no idea how soon we will get anything to eat. We have not felt hunger since we have had so much excitement.

The white women are very much pleased with their present situation. When they were taken to see the chiefs Mrs. Morgan tried to get Col. Moore's revolver to shoot Big Head, and said he was the worst Indian in the whole tribe. The women tried to escape in November but it snowed in the night and their tracks were followed and they were captured the next afternoon, and had to ride back behind their captors. Their feet were so sore and lacerated from traveling all night that they suffered great pain for many days, so they did not try to escape again.

It is said that Mrs. Morgan has not even smiled since she has been released from captivity, while Miss White is becoming quite cheerful. Dan Brewster has sworn vengeance on the Indians for the rough treatment of his sister. He looks as though he would do what he made up his mind to do. He is not very talkative, but I had a friendly chat with him and he told me a lot about his Kansas experience and his claim on the Solomon.

Sunday, March 21, 1869

We were all ready to march at daylight when a troop of Indians came bearing a white flag and wanted one more talk with the "White Chief." It was the last effort to secure the release of their chiefs. They made all kinds of promises and were willing to give any security they had if Custer would set them at liberty. They were told that it was an impossibility, but if the tribe would go on a reservation and be peaceable they would be set free and also the woman and children captured at the fight on November 27 last. Also that the prisoners would be well treated if they did not try to escape. Three months would give them time to all get in around Camp Supply and when they had done so, all the prisoners held by the Government would be released and taken to Camp Supply and given their freedom. They finally departed apparently satisfied and said they would soon be on the reservation.

Then the command started toward the north and by night came to what was called Sergeant Major Creek, a branch of the Washita, where we went into camp.

When a mule or horse gives out he is shot, and when there was an opportunity the boys would cut out a piece of the flesh, even if it were very poor, and take it with them. After we were in camp I took a stroll to where my company was camped and some of the boys were cooking mule meat. We had been to see Sergt. Mather and he told us there was nothing in the wagons to eat and we would have to get along the best we could until we arrived at the camp on the Washita.

Some of the boys said mule meat was as good as beef, and wanted me to taste it, but it had not been salted and I could not eat it. Perhaps it was because I knew what it was and it made me feel sick. I then went up to Capt. Finch's mess and they were just eating the last they had and I told him the boys were eating mule meat. The captain asked if I liked it. I told him I had tasted it, but could not eat it. He offered me over half of what he had left, but I refused. He insisted so hard, I ate a bite or two and as they had so little I would eat no more.

Our squad is pretty small now, George Vann, Ingleman and myself, and we are with our companies most of the time during the day, but stay with the wagons at night. I spent an hour visiting my cousin this evening and he said Dan Brewster was with his sister most of the time, as he was only a substitute teamster and had no team to look after. We have quite a large wagon train, but kill some disabled mules every day.

The Government does not own any of the train, but contractors furnish the train wagons and mules to transport Government property, and the wagons and mules destroyed are not any loss to the Government. The teamsters are well supplied with provisions for the trip before they start out, and it is surmised much of the stores taken and laid to the soldiers, was taken to keep up their larder.

Monday, March 22, 1869

It has been a cold night, but is cloudy this morning. We are in marching order by daylight and our course is down the creek toward the Washita. We are in a poor condition to stand very much cold as there are only three of us and have but three blankets between us, and no tent, so sleep under a wagon. We were pretty cold all night, but slept most of the time. We know that there are plenty of provisions, blankets and clothing not very far ahead and all are very anxious to get there.

There was quite an excitement among the men this morning. Someone had stolen the train master's riding mule during the night for he could not find it. He was a fat, sleek animal and would make much better eating than those poor, starved mules, so he thinks his mount was killed and eaten by some of the soldiers. If they did it they covered up the evidence, for hide or hair of it could not be found. He went around cursing everybody and offered a big sum if anyone would show him who took his mule. No one was even cooking mule meat. If he came near any of the companies the boys would jeer him, which made him all the worse. I feel like I would like something to eat.

We camp tonight again on Sergeant Major Creek, but we can see a line of timber a few miles ahead and we think it is the Washita and only a very few miles from the camp we are looking for.

I got a little salt from my cousin and tried to eat mule meat, but it did not take much to do me, for I was sick for a while. As the Washita cannot be much farther, we are contemplating getting up early and when the camp guard is being called in, to slip out and hurry to the Washita and follow that stream, until we find the camp. The troopers are going too slow for us as they have to keep with the train of wagons.

If we get started before the advance guard we can keep ahead of them. We are now sure we can find the train for we have only to follow the river. If we fail we can return to the wagon trail and follow it until we catch up. So, we have decided to make a trial. We have been assured that this creek flows into the Washita, so we will cut across the country to the timber on our right which is pretty heavy and must be along a large stream.

The mules are giving out much faster than the horses. We seldom see a horse and they are in advance but we often see a team with a mule refusing to go and it is taken out and shot, and the wagon goes on with four mules instead of six, or another is put in his place after a wagon is abandoned and burned.

Tuesday, March 23, 1869

We are up before daylight and all ready to start out as soon as the bugle calls in the pickets who come in and get their breakfast, when they have anything to eat.

Finally recall sounded and we were near the picket line and hid until they passed, when we pulled out as fast as we could walk and it was not long until we had left the camp some distance behind. We felt like deserters, but we were going for something to eat, and when we got it we would take our places again. We saw some prairie dogs, some quail and a cottontail or two but we were not looking for game and we did not want to shoot for some scout might be near and take us back to the regiment.

About 9 o'clock we came to what we supposed to be the Washita for it was the largest stream we had seen since we crossed the North Fork of Red River a day before we captured the Indians. We followed down the south or right bank, keeping near the timber. Finally we decided we were likely to pass the train, for they might be camped on the other side, so we went in close to the stream, when about 3 o'clock we came to a place where we found piles of animal bones. There were so many bones that we concluded it must be where Gen. Custer had his fight with Black Kettle and the bones were those of the several hundred Indian ponies killed after the fight. Then we looked around for some time to see if we could see anything else that indicated a fight. I found a broken revolver quite rusty and a few marks on trees and finally decided it was where the fight took place, and near which the wagon train and the rest of the regiment were to meet.

We started on, and had only gone a little distance when we came to a place where some logs and limbs had been placed around a couple of mounds. Here then was the place where Maj. Elliott and the nineteen troopers had been buried. Then we knew for sure we were on the right road. We then started on and soon met a trooper on horseback who was much surprised to see us. We asked the first thing if he had anything to eat with him. He said no, but there was plenty a mile below here. Then Gus asked him if he had any tobacco, so he gave Gus a cigar which he broke in two pieces and handed one to me. I put it in my mouth and chewed it, and for a wonder it tasted good and did not make me sick. We then hurried along and soon came to the camp where we hunted up our separate companies.

As soon as I got to my company the boys all came to say "Hello," and asked all kinds of questions. They had heard nothing of us and some of them said they never expected to see us again. They could not understand how we came to be the only ones saved alive, and I had to explain it all to them. I told them I had lived on air and water for a couple of weeks and would like something to eat. They soon had plenty before me but I could only eat a cracker and drink a cup of coffee and that was enough to make me sick for a while. Frank Doty and Bill Radenbocker took me to their tent and wanted to know so many things that I gave them my diary and went to sleep.

Wednesday, March 24, 1869

The command got in last night after dark, but the wagon train did not arrive until about 10 o'clock this forenoon. I slept pretty late and ate a little breakfast and had the best cup of coffee I ever drank in my life.

After breakfast I had to tell the boys all about the trip and about the women taken from the Indians. I could not answer all the questions, so told them to let me tell them all about it and referred to my notes so would not miss anything. As Frank and Bill had read it all they helped me out from what they could remember.

I never did so much talking in all my life. The other boys who were along could not tell much except they were so tired and had so little to eat that it affected their memory, and they did not know whether they were dead or alive.

About sixty wagons left here yesterday after more provisions to be brought from Camp Supply. "Major" Inman, as he is called, but he is only an army contractor, sent a courier last night after the train to have them return as the horses and mules we have cannot be expected to haul even the empty wagons. The boys here have tents and more baggage than we had in both regiments, when we came in from the campaign.

A good many of the boys are sick today from overeating, but I have profited by my former experience when we first arrived at Camp Supply, so am only eating a cracker an hour, and then I am more hungry than when I first came in. I drank a lot of coffee though. I am staying with the boys now and our squad have naturally gone to their companies, but we are at liberty to get together again and may do so.

I will consult Sergt. Mather and he may need us, and if so we would not have to be detailed as we are supposed to be on duty when there is any duty to do. He told me once that if they ever had full rations to issue again he would like for me to help him as a permanent detail, which I will be very much pleased to do.

The wagon train called back from en route to Camp Supply came in this evening for they had only been gone one day. It has been raining all day, and is quite muddy. Doty and Bill seem never to get tired asking questions. When any of the other boys come to see me they tell them I am sick and don't want to be disturbed. Capt. Finch came to see me, saying he heard I was sick, but I told him I was feeling pretty good now.

When I went up to the company officers' tents Lieut. Stoddard shook hands with me and was very friendly and hoped that when we became citizens again we would hold no animosity toward each other. I told him I had no grudge against him, but I did not trust him because he had told me if I would enlist I should be company clerk and do no guard duty, but when he had gone to the adjutant and had me taken off the detail as company clerk, so I would have to do a common soldier's duty, I had lost confidence in him as an honorable man, while Capt. Finch had been my best friend and I would always honor him for it.

It is nearly a mile up to the spot called the battle field where I had picked up the old revolver, which is worthless. I traded for another Colt's revolver, but broken, and am going to keep it to take home. One of the boys had a good Remington revolver he said he would give me, for he did not want to carry it, so now I have two revolvers to carry, one a good one, but I have no cartridges for it. All the boys are anxious to see the captives, the Kansas women who are with our regimental officers and the Indians who are with the Seventh.

If we stay here tomorrow I want to go up and see the "battle ground" so I can tell more about it. Many of the boys who came across from North Fork have visited the battle ground, and had three weeks of picnic compared to what some of us had. We are camped in the valley near the river and a couple of hundred yards from the road we made on the way down to Fort Cobb. The rain did not stop the men from loading our plunder on the wagons to be taken to Camp Supply.

Thursday, March 25, 1869

We are still in camp for the train did not get ready to start and they thought a day's rest for horses and mules would be better than to hurry them too fast. A good many of the boys are quite sick and are in care of the doctors.

I continue my cracker-an-hour diet and do not feel any bad effects. Tomorrow I will take a cracker every half hour for a while. While I feel pretty well I am weak, or feel so. I went to see Adj. Steele and he gave me a pass to go up to the battle ground today. Quite a good many are going from both regiments.

While looking for information about the fight one of the Seventh boys who was in the fight offered to tell us what he had seen and the location of the camp. Most of the tents were on the north side of the stream. There was one large tent used for a storehouse for any kind of property the Indians were not using—saddles and robes, tent poles, dried meats, ammunition and all their extra stores. He also showed us where the tent of Black Kettle, the chief, stood, also a tree behind which a squaw had a little white boy, and when she saw he was discovered and could not escape she plunged a knife into the little fellow and killed him.*   The soldier who saw her do it, shot her on the spot.†   When the troops came back ten days later they looked for the bodies, but all had been taken away.

We also saw the pile of ashes where all the wigwams were burned.   There were a lot of poles in the warehouse, but all went up in smoke.   It was all snow covered when the fight occurred, but now it was all gone and green grass has appeared.   We could still see the bones of the ponies across the creek, so we passed quite near the spot of the Indian camp and did not know it.   Many places were shown us where something or another took place, and how the attack was made, so it has been a day few of us will ever forget.

Friday, March 26, 1869

We are up early and have our breakfast before daylight. We are going home, but do not get started before 9 o'clock. It is a warm, pleasant day and occasionally the boys of our regiment cheer, as they expect to keep doing until we are mustered out of the service.   I am now with the company and will have to do duty like the rest if I am called upon unless Capt. Finch calls me to do some clerical work for him or has me detailed for some service that will excuse me.

After marching fifteen miles we came to the South Canadian and camped on nearly the same spot that we occupied on our way down.   Everything looks familiar around here.   Before crossing the river I went for a couple of hun-

---

*This little boy was Willie Blynn, who, with his mother, Mrs. Clara Blynn, had been captured by the Cheyennes several weeks previously.   The mother was killed by the savages when Custer attacked the village and before she could be rescued.

†T. P. Lyon, of Los Angeles, a trooper in the 7th Cavalry on the Washita campaign, told the editor of this diary that he witnessed the murder of the little Blynn boy, and shot the squaw.

dred yards up a small creek that emptied into the river and saw where the waters had washed under a bank so it had caved down, leaving a perpendicular wall which presented a most curious formation. There was about six feet of clay there, a layer of bright red brown and gray from six inches to two feet thick. I never saw anything like it before and would have liked to have called the attention of the other boys to it, so I gathered samples of each until my pockets were full. Then I started to cross the river. It appeared to be from one inch to two feet deep and quite wide, so I rolled up my pants as high as I could and took my boots in one hand and gun in the other, and stepped in. It went over my head for I had stepped in a washout about three feet deep. I tried to keep my gun above water, but it was thoroughly wet, as were my shoes and clothes. When I got up I went across all right and did not find another place over a foot deep. I think I must have found the deepest spot and "put my foot in it." The river bed was fully 200 yards wide and nearly all the way across was covered with water of different depths.

I spent a whole evening drying my clothes by a good hot fire and as I have to go on guard at 10 o'clock I have them very near dry by that time. There is plenty of dry driftwood and tall grass. We are having plenty to eat and I am still dieting to a short ration of meat, crackers and coffee. The boys have pulled a lot of dead grass for our bed tonight which I will enjoy after midnight. There is no timber along the river here except occasionally a small cottonwood. We have not seen any place where the land is rich to be compared to Cache Creek.

We have seen no buffaloes for months and we will be glad when we get up into Kansas again when we can have all the fresh meat we can eat.

Saturday, March 27, 1869

We are on our way as soon as we can see the trail and expect to reach the North Canadian tonight for the boys do not seem to get tired and keep close behind the cavalry. They do not forget to cheer once in a while. We are marching over the same route we made last fall when I was flank patrol and then detailed as guard over the provision wagons.

Today I ate all I wanted for the first time and tonight I did not want anything to eat. We ate dinner or lunch at Mulberry Creek, where we stopped an hour this afternoon. We marched fifteen miles and camped beside a pond in a large hardpan hole, as it is rock or hardpan and no grass.

The horses and mules soon had the water so mixed up that no one could drink it for mules and horses were all over it, so it was not fit to use. We got a pail full near the edge which we strained several times and made some coffee. We are now getting so close to Camp Supply that we can hardly wait and do not get to sleep very soon for we expect to hear good news from home. I am not very enthusiastic on that account for no one that I know is aware of my whereabouts as I have not sent a letter to anyone since we left Fort Cobb, because I had nothing with which to buy material.

Sunday, March 28, 1869

I am feeling fine this morning and it is a very pleasant day. My appetite is not first rate yet and I only drink a cup of coffee with a hardtack and fall in line with the rest. We reach the North Canadian just before noon and stop an hour to eat. We never have stopped to eat at noon before except yesterday and today. There is good water, good wood and good grass, so it is a good place to stop for an hour or so to eat our good dinner, and we are making good use of them all.

We still see the little oaks a few inches high with acorns on them. The grass along the river is called buffalo grass and the horses and mules seem to like it even if it is dead.

It is about 5 o'clock when we reach Camp Supply. We go into camp in the same place we occupied when we were here last. Everyone is cheerful and glad to get back here but we are not expecting to go back home the way we came nor have the experiences we had to get here. A few of our boys who were left here when we went south, were out to meet us, but Lieut. Tilton and the rest are now at Fort Dodge where they are serving as guards to trains or pickets for the fort. Maj. Dimon is still here in charge, but some one else will now have to take his position for he will go north with the regiment. The Indian prisoners will go to Fort Hays.

Monday, March 29, 1869

We did not get up this morning until nearly daylight and we did not hear a bugle call, which is rather unusual for us, and as we needed the rest, everyone was given that privilege so were not called. We are still 200 miles from Fort Hays where we are to be discharged, and are very anxious to be on our way.

Our officers draw rations to be for the trip north and we draw rations of soap so we can clean up and wash our clothes and blankets for we surely need a good scrubbing. This is the first time we have had a chance to wash our clothes and bedding for a month or more, so we make good use of this opportunity.

This evening we go around to take a look at each other and I hardly recognized some of the boys. They really looked like dudes with their hair cut and parted in the middle—and the strut they put on!

The horses used by the boys were turned over to the 7th Cavalry and the boys will have to walk the last 200 miles like the rest of us. We expect to start north in the morning. The evening is spent telling experiences. The men here have been guarding trains from Fort Dodge, and some of them were down to Maj. Inman's camp on the Washita the first trip. We leave in the morning.

Tuesday; March 30, 1869

Reveille at 4 o'clock and no one has to be pulled out of bed, and we are all ready to march long before daylight, but do not get started before 6. It is ninety miles to Fort Dodge, and we expect to make it in three days. It is the nearest fort and almost direct to Fort Hays. It is on the Arkansas River in Southern Kansas. We march fifteen miles and stop for dinner or lunch at Beaver Creek.

We have no roads to make for they are already made and in excellent condition. After lunch we marched eight miles and camp on a small creek where there are no trees but driftwood enough is found to get our meals. Those who did not have wood gathered buffalo chips, so all had a good supper.

We are having plenty eats now and all are feeling fine and spend the evening singing and cheering. I never heard the singing in camp that there is tonight. The Indians brought from the Sweetwater, or Elk Creek, are still with the 7th Cavalry and the women with us. Miss White is looking much better, but Mrs. Morgan has not made much improvement and has very little to say to anyone. Miss White is much more cheerful and smiles occasionally and both hope to meet their families or friends in the near future. I saw Brewster a couple of times, but did not get to talk to him. He was with the train.

Wednesday, March 31, 1869

We get started at daylight and soon pass a place where Company M boys tell us two scouts were killed by the Indians about a year ago. They were on their way south carrying the mail and when the Indians became too many for them, they killed their horses and took refuge behind their dead bodies. When found later by their friends they were dead and horribly mutilated. Quite a pile of empty shells showed they must have sold their lives dearly and had perhaps killed several Indians.

We stopped for lunch at the Cimarron River. There is considerable alkali in the water, so it did not taste very good. We camp for the night on Crooked Creek where there is plenty of wood and water with no alkali, so we have a good supper and the boys do not seem to get tired cheering for they break out every once in a while. Even after they are in bed some one will give a yell and then others will repeat. It is rather annoying if we want to go to sleep. I have not heard how many miles we have come today, but it is going to take us four days to get to Fort Dodge.

We cannot go any faster than the cavalry, so we have to stay with them, but perhaps they do not know that we are in a hurry to get to see our folks.

Thursday, April 1, 1869

Everybody turns out early now, so we are always ready when the bugle sounds the march. Our sergeant major, G. G. Gunning, and Lieut. Brady of Company E had some trouble today and the sergeant major was reduced to the ranks. The fuss was over something that took place on the evening of the day we left Topeka. Brady claimed that Gunning returned the first night with others, to attend a dance for the benefit of the officers, then leaving. Lieut. Brady did not go back, and claimed that Gunning

BIG TREE, KIOWA CHIEF, SENT TO THE HUNTSVILLE, TEXAS, PENI-
TENTIARY FOR LIFE FOR HIS PART IN THE MASSACRE AT
SALT CREEK PRAIRIE, TEXAS

—From the Collection of E. A. Brininstool.

represented him by telling someone he was Lieut. Brady. They were separated, but they both say it is not settled yet.

We are now where there are pretty fresh signs of buffaloes and hunters were out looking for them, but none were brought in. We stopped for lunch on Bluff Creek. The 7th Cavalry had a camp on this creek for a couple of weeks last fall. After an hour's rest we started out on our journey again and camp for the night on a small creek with only a few scattering cottonwood trees. It is pretty cold and windy and nothing but driftwood and that has nearly all been taken before we came. Some of the boys have gone one mile up and down the creek for wood.

We only make one big fire in our company after supper, but soon go to bed. We sleep four in a bed so we will have plenty of blankets over us. We have grass under us.

Friday, April 2, 1869

It was still cold and windy this morning, but we were "ready to go" when the bugle sounded. The Seventh always takes the lead and they still have the Indian prisoners with the officers at the head of the command. We have an ambulance at our head in which the two women ride. We stop for dinner every day now and today we halt for an hour at Mulberry Creek, nine miles from Fort Dodge. There are a good many trees here and we are protected from the wind while we eat our lunch.

As we have only a few miles to go this afternoon and have plenty of time to make it, we do not hurry to leave here while the wind blows so hard on the open plains. We arrive at Fort Dodge about 4 o'clock and go into camp outside the stockade, northeast of the fort. The Regulars go inside and have quarters in the building. There seems to be quite a town along the river, some very substantial houses and a good many cheap ones. Inside the stockade there are some very nice Government buildings with officers' and soldiers' quarters.

We were not allowed to go inside the stockade, but a good many of our officers spent the evening in the town. They came into camp all hours of the night and it sounded like some were drunk.

Saturday, April 3, 1869

We do not march today because the Seventh have a good place to stay and do not care to leave so soon, consequently we have to await their pleasure. We have come 110 miles from Camp Supply and it is 90 miles to Fort Hays. There is only a small garrison at the fort. Lieut. Tilton has been here for some time on duty in and around the fort, also in command of escorts for trains to and from Camp Supply. Some of our company boys have been here also. All of them will go with us to Fort Hays and a part of the Seventh will relieve them.

There are a good many scouts here now who carry mail in all directions and to other forts. All are in the employ of the Government. Some carry messages to different commanders of posts on the frontier. Some of these are skilled in riding by and shooting at a target while their horses and ponies are on the run. They hit the mark while the horse is on a run, and shooting under the horse's neck while hanging on his side and some picked hats off the ground while on the run. They rode in every kind of position you could imagine.

Lieut. Tilton has been kept pretty busy since we left him here. He tells us some of his experiences and what he has seen while here. He and Lieut. Gordon of Company H have been good friends and shared their duties together most of the time. The buffaloes have come close to the fort a couple of times during the winter. Lieut. Tilton tells us the picket posts around the fort consist of holes in the ground 6 x 6 and 5 feet deep so the picket can stand in them and see over the top in all directions. At the same time he can have a fire on the bottom or floor which cannot be seen, and the sentry can keep his feet warm and be protected from the wind day and night.

Lieut. Tilton told me he was officer of the guard one night and went around to see that all were on duty, when he found one man so interested in a letter he was reading by the light of his fire he did not hear the officer's approach and on looking in on him discovered the sentry's gun leaning against the wall behind him. Tilton quietly reached down and took the gun and then spoke to him. Imagine his surprise when he found he had been caught on duty unarmed. That guard was most severely reprimanded after being shown what the result could be if an Indian had taken his gun and he could not have given an alarm, thereby putting the fort and all its inmates in danger of capture. He was finally given his gun again but that picket felt his disgrace so keenly that he soon after deserted.

We also hear from the boys' description of their scouting trips and some of them went south with the first provision train to Inman Camp on the Washita.

We drew rations this forenoon and have a big feed of beans, which just suited me. I do not care for rice. Some of the men went over to the town and are coming into camp drunk. They are pretty noisy sometimes and some are quarrelsome and have to be placed under arrest. In order to stop the noise and racket we are ordered to march at 2 o'clock so as to get away from the saloons and keep the men from getting into trouble.

We march fourteen miles and camp on Sawlog Creek. The noisy ones have become quiet by the time we are ready to retire. There is hardly any timber along this creek and when told it was Sawlog Creek we naturally looked for saw-logs. Perhaps the timber had been made into sawlogs.

Sunday, April 4, 1869

We were very much surprised when we woke up this morning and found it snowing, for we had begun to think the winter was over. It was the first snow we had seen for a month, but we started out just the same as if it had been a pleasant day. We stop for lunch at a small stream flowing into the Middle Fork of Pawnee River where there has been a good camping ground for those gone before.

We camp for the night on the North Fork of the Pawnee after a march of twenty-six miles. The soil along this stream is the richest since we left Cache Creek. All the afternoon we have been going over a rich, black sandy loam and sunflowers on both sides of the road from ten to fifteen feet high. About 10 o'clock we were going by a mound with some brush on it, when suddenly about twenty soldiers came up out of the mound and we learned they were living in a dugout. It was quite different from the dugouts we had down at Fort Cobb and Cache Creek. Theirs was a long, large and deep trench covered with logs, grass and dirt. We did not go inside of it but some of the boys had been in them and knew how they were made. They are quite warm and comfortable in winter and also cool in summer.

We did not have an invitation to take a look at this one but have the opportunity some other time and place. We are told that many of the settlers on the frontier live in dugouts of this kind and have a guard house near the living room in which they can retire and from loopholes can see and shoot the attacking Indians and not be in much danger of being killed. Indians do not attack settlers living in dugouts, so I am told by those who have been in them.

Monday, April 5, 1869

Reveille at 4 o'clock and every one is ready to start when the Seventh takes the lead. All the boys are anxious to be on the road. Some have sore feet, but manage to hobble along and are always on hand at meal time. When we stop for lunch at noon we have gone eighteen miles. When we go into camp at night on Walnut Creek we have gone thirty miles and few complain of being tired. Several of the boys, especially the fleshy ones, complain of being tired but I stand it pretty well as my feet are in good condition and have been so all our trip of several hundred miles.

We left the Pawnee River soon after we started. Some day that part of Kansas will be the garden spot of the state. I may come back here in the near future and take up a claim for I am sure I could not find a better place in the state.

We camp near the stream, but have to hunt for wood, which is very scarce. There are no trees except a cottonwood or two, which are only scrubs. It is a mystery how it got the name of Walnut Creek. I am getting as anxious as anyone to get to our destination. I have not heard from home for so long I want to get where I can write home and get letters. I do not regret my experience, but am glad it is so near over. I surely have something to remember in future years.

Tuesday, April 6, 1869

We do not start so early this morning as we are only twelve miles from Fort Hays. The cavalry went on to the fort last night and some of our officers went with them and will select a nice camping place for us when we arrive. We will have to stay there several days before we can be mustered out and I will likely be called or detailed to close up the accounts of the company with the Government. The mail carrier went through to Fort Dodge and left mail for our regiment, but I got nothing. Mail goes to Fort Dodge twice a week.

I heard today that Mrs. Morgan's husband met her at Fort Dodge. He has not fully recovered from his wound and has to use crutches. They went with our officers to Fort Hays last night. Miss White hopes to meet some of her family if they are alive. She does not know but what all were killed. It is said Mrs. Morgan was greatly excited when she met her husband. She did not know but he had been killed until informed of his escape by her brother, Daniel Arthur Brewster, who has traveled with them ever since they left Camp Supply. Although I have looked for him several times I did not find him anywhere among the wagons going to Fort Hays. We are getting too anxious to go to sleep now.

Wednesday, April 7, 1869

We start this morning as soon as we can see the road and reach our destination long before noon and go into camp at the junction of Big Creek with Kaw River. We can see Fort Hays west of us and Hays City across the river from our camp. We can also see the railroad trains coming and going, and we would be glad if we were aboard one going east. We camped in a nice grove of cottonwoods and the ground is covered with tall grass, so there is no danger of mud for a while.

We expect to be here about ten days as it will be that long before all the reports are in, for we have much property to account for during our service. We did not turn in half the horses we received and every horse has to be accounted for, as well as saddles, bridles, lariats, saddle blankets, etc. Now we are having to turn in our guns, cartridges, belts, blankets, etc., or account for all that is missing. If the men cannot tell what became of property in their possession they may have to pay for it, or have it taken out of the few dollars coming to them.

We draw "A" tents for we have been a couple of months without shelter of any kind. It is windy here and the tents are greatly appreciated. A good many of the boys have gone over to the town tonight and some of them may never come back again.

Thursday, April 8, 1869

We have had a good rest and I wanted to go over to the city today and see how it looked in civilization once more, but Capt. Finch came and informed me that I had been detailed for company clerk and he wanted me to assist him in making out the company reports. I go up to his tent and find a pile of blank reports to fill out.

Lieut. Tilton and I will have to do the writing while Capt. Finch and Lieut. Stoddard will hunt for information whenever needed in making the reports. An officer has explained to us what is required, so we fully understand the blanks and what we are to write in them. He will stay at our headquarters so we can consult him when we do not fully understand anything we come across in any of the blank reports. We have made a list of all we have to do and tomorrow will get to work at the beginning.

We have a very nice camp here with good water and plenty to eat. Uncle Sam must be trying to atone for the way he has treated us since we enlisted. We were presented to him by Governor Crawford and we perhaps were not much appreciated or he would have fed us better and treated us like Americans.

The boys have nothing whatever to do and are making lots of noise. Those who went over to town are coming in pretty drunk. They have no money yet, still they can get whisky "without money and without price." They say whisky is as free as water over there. Tilton and I spend the evening going over the blanks so as to be more familiar with them and make no mistakes. We have to make out most of them in duplicate, so we are going to make out one and be sure it is correct and then copy it for the Government.

Friday, April 9, 1869

We have our breakfast early and I report for duty and find Lieut. Tilton already on hand. We are going to have quite a job on our hands for we have no records of any kind since we left Topeka. I am filling out blanks from the captain's memory, and he is not sure he is right all the time. He has not even a memorandum of anything and we have to report all lost property beginning with the horses and we only turned in a few more than half of them. The missing ones will be reported in various ways—some stolen by deserters, some lost in a stampede, some frozen to death, and some condemned and shot. The men have to be consulted to know just how each one has to be classified. The deserters generally took their horses and equipment.

I have learned that I was detailed as clerk and never returned to duty as I supposed, so I have been accusing Lieut. Stoddard wrongfully, for he gave an order for me to be placed in the ranks, which he had no authority to do while I was detailed for a special purpose. The adjutant informed me today that I was still company clerk and had been all the time. I also had been detailed for duty in the commissary and if I could fill both positions no one could change the details except through his office.

I quit about 4 o'clock today and took a stroll over the camp and called on George Vann and Gus Ingleman. Lieut. Tilton went over to town for a while and wanted me to go along. I heard such hard tales about what is going on over there that I do not think it a very safe place to go even if you mind your own business. There is more noise tonight than ever. A good many of them have come _|home from town and have been drinking but how they got it I don't know, for none of the men have been paid, so have no money to spend, yet.

Saturday,. April 10, 1869

It is pleasant this morning and some of the boys go hunting, but there is nothing to kill for miles as the buffaloes have been driven out of the country by hunters from all over the East. This is the place where William F. Cody received the name of "Buffalo Bill." He was the man who supplied the Kansas Pacific with meat when the road was being built through here. We have a camp guard, but they can't see very well as any one can get out or in, when they are not looking toward them. If there were no guard half the regiment would be gone and we would have a hard time getting information we need from the men regarding the property issued to them.

There are several officers here from the fort who are always ready to give instructions how to proceed if we are in doubt. We have to make out a monthly clothing report and we have no records of ever having received any clothing, so they give us the Government records and we have to accept their figures as correct.

We find it slow work for we have to depend on the fort officers so much, and they do not work very long hours. They give us a task to do until they come back. We take a couple of hours' recess from 5 to 7 for we are not used to this kind of work. Capt. Finch and Lieut. Stoddard are busy getting affidavits from the men and they often have a hard time to find them.

The boys who have been over to town tell us that the women we rescued from the Indians have gone. Mrs. Morgan and her husband went with D. A. Brewster to their claims. No one was here to meet Miss White and she was sent to relatives in the East. She believes now her people were all killed.

The boys are coming in tonight as noisy as every night. Some of them have been in a fight as their faces are badly discolored and their clothing covered with blood. They say some of them were not able to get back to camp and will have to sober up in the city bastile. Everyone says it is a hard place, and all have to keep together for protection or be killed.

Sunday, April 11, 1869

It has been a very cold and disagreeable day but we have secured a sheet-iron stove for our tent which is so comfortable we do not feel the cold. We have to call the boys who have lost Government property, such as horses and equipment, guns, tents, etc., to make affidavits as to how they lost or disposed of them. I am kept busy all day making out their affidavits and getting their signatures. There will be quite a number that the captain will have to sign as "property taken by deserters." Nearly all those who deserted took their horses and their equipment, and in some cases property belonging to others. All of them took their guns, blankets and clothing, dog tents or anything they expected to need. Some of the men had no use for a gun or anything else if they had to carry them. These were reported as lost or taken by deserters. I do not think all the property charged to deserters was really taken by them, but that seemed the easiest way to allow for it.

Tonight Sergt. David Dougherty came in from town with both eyes blackened. He is a half-blood Indian, large and strong, and weighs 200 pounds or more. I asked him why he let anyone beat him that way. He said several jumped on him at once and while they were blacking his eyes he was getting their money and he showed me a big handful of bills he had. Said he thinks he got all they had. After he hit one he had no trouble in getting his money.

Monday, April 12, 1869

It has stopped raining but is still cold and windy. Those who were over to town last night brought in a good supply of whisky and the guards are treated as they pass until they are not fit for duty in a short time. The camp is a noisy place after midnight and they are not entirely quiet at daylight. I have never seen so many drunken men at one time before. More than half the regiment do not care to go to town and like myself have never been over yet. There is fighting and shooting every day and night and the city officers do not arrest anybody, so I hear. The boys have all they can eat and are getting indolent and lazy.

We have finished the clothing reports. Our next work will be the general expense reports. The boys will next turn in all property they have on hand, and it will be listed and credited to them. I take an hour off at noon and two off from 5 to 7, and then work until quite late. Capt. Finch or Lieut. Stoddard brings us in a lunch about 9 which we appreciate very much. We then work another hour for we want to get the job off our hands as soon as possible. The tent in which we are working is a large wall tent, 12 x 16. We have a long table in the middle. We find out through the officers from the fort that all the other companies are without any records and have the same trouble making out their reports as we do.

Tuesday, April 13, 1869

The men were called in line this morning and told to clean up their guns ready to be turned in. A list of the men was made and they were credited with their guns, belts, cartridge holders, etc., as their names were called. It was after noon when we were through. Fourteen of our company had deserted and that many guns were charged to deserters. Several had no guns and had to make an affidavit for their loss. After we are through with the men we have to fill out the blanks for the property turned in, and also for property lost and how lost.

It is windy here most of the time, but comfortable inside our tents.

Lieut. Tilton and I take a walk this evening and go up to the fort, which is about a mile up the river and on the opposite side from the city. It is quite a large building inside a stockade enclosing fifteen or twenty acres. There are houses and quarters for officers and families, also others for men. Some of the officers have a flower garden and lawn. We do not go inside the residence portion but along the barracks, where the men of the 7th Cavalry are now quartered. We do not get back to our camp until it is almost dark and the boys have eaten supper. The camp is as noisy as ever.

Wednesday, April 14, 1869

It is very cold and windy this morning and someone has to keep our little stove red hot to make it comfortable. We are getting along fine with our reports. Some of the affidavits and entries are really comical. When the men had to account for their dog tents, one fellow said his feet hurt him so he could hardly walk, so he threw his boots away and wrapped his feet in pieces of tent. Another said his horse was so very hungry and he could find nothing but snow for him to eat, so he fed him his tent as he had no poles for it. Any kind of excuse seems to go. If all these reports have to be sent to Washington for examination before we get any pay we will not have money enough to take us home. Capt. Finch said he made a great mistake by not keeping me on the job all the time, keeping a record of what the men received that has to be accounted for.

Now the officers have to swear that these records are correct, but only to the best of their knowledge and belief, which they can easily do, for they know nothing about so many things, so they only believe what has been told or surmised.

I have been all afternoon making out ordnance reports, accounting for our ammunition. Most of it was for hunting and shooting at marks but it went for "practice," so that was all there was to it. We have been working pretty steady all day and it is late when we stop. I did not get to bed until after 12.

Thursday, April 15, 1869

I do not get up this morning until after the boys had eaten breakfast but they left me all I cared most for—a cup of coffee. It is not very cold this morning and the sun came out after 8 and has been shining most of the day.

The noise in camp last night did not keep me awake. The effects of last night are plainly visible for there are many discolored faces and eyes in camp. It is a fight nearly every night—citizens vs. soldiers. Sometimes the citizens get together and clean out the soldiers by small squads, and keep them from uniting. Perhaps the next night the soldiers will get in a body and run every man in citizens' clothes out of town or disarm them and shut them up. In any case it is not safe anywhere in town after dark and most of our boys are not wanting to go home with a black eye or a broken limb, so they stay in camp.

The Government officers who have been here to give us assistance have examined our reports and say they are satisfactory, which we were very glad to know although I would not want to swear to some of the entries in them. Everything has been accepted so far and we are getting along fine, and hope the rest will be much easier since all property is disposed of.

Friday, April 16, 1869

The stormy weather seems to be over now and it is more like spring. We have no need for fire today. We hope to be ready to muster out by Monday. I spent the day writing out discharges, which the captain will have to sign. These, with the muster rolls and pay rolls, will go in with the paymaster at the fort and we will have to appear there and get our money and receipt for it. We are told tonight that we have done all that is required of us, so we can go and get our pay. Some of us will be very glad to have a little money once more. We have never had a cent that was due us since we were mustered into the service.

I don't know if we would have ever gotten any pay had it not been for Gen. Sheridan and Col. Crawford going to Washington and laying the matter before Congress assembled there and seemingly unconscious of our existence.

Everyone who could be induced to go, went over to town this afternoon with the intention of cleaning up the roughs who had beaten some of our men so badly a few nights ago. They have been fighting every night more or less and the stronger party is victorious. The roughs knock down and rob any soldier they can catch alone, be it Regular or Volunteer. The boys are going in a body and clean them out of town.

Saturday, April 17, 1869

I did not get up very early, only in time to eat breakfast with the rest. The boys came home from town after an all-night carousal. Some were almost crazy drunk and had to be put under arrest and even tied up to trees or posts. They did not have any trouble all night but had their own way. The rough citizens kept under cover and did not show themselves at all.

The regiment was mustered out this afternoon and the boys are glad they are citizens again. They cannot keep still, but keep cheering. They have plenty of the crazy water, and the effect is seen in a good many of them.

My work is completed and I have nothing to do. I met Sergt. David Dougherty, the half-breed Shawnee Indian of our company, and he had his pockets full of bills. He said three roughs met him and attempted to rob him. Two of them made a grab for him and with one hand he stretched them out and held them, and with the other took their money and let them go and he beat it. Then he went through the others, who had not revived, and he then had an inventory and found he had cleaned up $115 in just a few minutes. Handing me a $5 bill he said, "Take this, and remember old Dave Dougherty." He was a jolly, good-natured Shawnee half-breed, well liked by all the men in the company. We had five Shawnees in the company.

Sunday, April 18, 1869

The boys did not have to listen for the bugle this morning for we are citizens again and we get into line again for the last time, and march over to the fort to draw our pay.

After we had arrived we had to await our turn. There was a company just ahead of us, so we had to stand in line for at least an hour which seemed like half a day. Companies A, D, F and G were paid off before us and have gone over to town to take the train which will carry them home.

As we march over to town we can see our camp with the tents still standing but not a soul is to be seen there. Just as we reached the bridge to cross over to town, Capt. Finch met us and informed us that there would not be a train to take us home until tomorrow, and advised us to go back to our camp and sleep in the tents tonight, which most of us would rather do than spend the night in town.

Doty, Radenbocker and I take our old tent and spend our last night in camp together. We lie awake until late, telling what we expect to do after we get home. These boys have been friends a long time and are going back to Missouri and perhaps get married and settle on a farm, for both have been raised in the country and like country life best, or much better than chasing after Indians.

As for myself I have had enough of the life of a soldier, although I regret nothing I have done and have had much experience that I will never forget. I am not very anxious to go on a claim on the frontier, for I have heard the experience of so many settlers that I do not really crave for that kind of a life at present.

I am satisfied now to go back to civilization and stay there, perhaps as long as I live. For the present I am going back to Springhill, see the friends there and then very likely go to my home in Logansport, Indiana. This has been my first experience away from home, as it is the first time I have been outside of the state of Indiana and was never absent from home more than a month before coming to Kansas.

Monday, April 19, 1869

It is another beautiful day and we have no rations, not even coffee, so will have to wait until we get over to town for our breakfast. I had filled out my discharge and Capt. Finch had signed it when it was sent to the paymaster. When we went to the office in the fort I stepped up to the window when my turn came and gave my name. My discharge and six months' pay were handed to me when I signed the receipt book opposite to my name. My discharge was signed by the paymaster.

Capt. Finch stayed with us here last night and this morning called us together and told us not to get scattered after going over to town or we would likely be robbed. Then he made quite a talk to us and hoped we would always be successful in whatever station of life we chose and above all to always remember our captain, who had a tender spot in his heart for every one of us. Then we all shook hands with him and several times he would wipe away a tear from his cheek, yet he was smiling all the while. Lieut. Tilton bade us all goodby and shook hands with all, wishing us all the good luck and happiness possible. Lieut. Stoddard went over town yesterday and we have not seen him and he may have gotten on the train and be on the way home now. After I have paid the boys all I owe them and get all coming to me I have $120. All I received from the Government was $96. Sergt. Streight paid me $20 he promised to give me in the horse trade made in Topeka and I never expected to get it for I thought he had forgotten it long ago. I would have never asked him for it, as we traded back later.

We started over to town about 9 o'clock and found the town full of people. About the first man I met was one of Company L's privates who asked me to keep his money. He wanted to get a drink and as he was a hard drinker he was afraid he would be robbed. He had only $35 left at that time, except perhaps some loose change, and was then pretty drunk. About 4 o'clock I ran across him and he was broke. Said he wanted $10 which I gave him and he went away and I saw him no more. I did not look for him either for he would have wanted to have the rest and lose it all.

We have been waiting all day for a train to come along to take us east. We had to wait an hour or more before we got our order for breakfast filled at the restaurant. Some of the boys could not wait and got a can of fruit at a grocery and ate it. While we were in a grocery a man bought a can of fruit and when he took out his purse to get the money to pay for it, a man behind reached over his shoulder and grabbed his purse and ran out of the door. Wiggs, the owner of the purse, took after him and they ran in front about 200 yards to the railroad track and then down the track, after him. It was about an even race, when Wiggs called out, "Stop or I'll shoot," but the man kept on and Wiggs shot four times before the man stopped and staggered, then fell dead. He was shot in the back. Wiggs was not even arrested as he had many witnesses to the robbery and the man still had his purse in his hand.

We are looking for a train all night and about 9 o'clock I put in an order for hot biscuits with butter and hot coffee, but there were so many orders ahead of me I did not get my meal until about 2 o'clock. This was the first meal of hot biscuits I had eaten for six months and they surely were delicious. My opinion is that the restaurant man thought I was filling all my pockets or had an elastic stomach for I did keep him busy for some time and he charged me one dollar.

Tuesday, April 20, 1869

A train arrived at 5 o'clock this morning and after waiting all night we picked up our baggage and got on. As I had eaten a late supper I did not get any breakfast. The train was so full a good many did not get seats and had to stand until some of the others got off at points nearest their homes.

We got started about daylight and the train followed the Kaw River all day. We did not see much timber until we came to Ellsworth and Junction City. We could see Fort Riley from the railroad not far from Junction City. We had passed few towns before. We did not see Gen. Custer before we left Hays City, and he may not have been there. Nor did Col. Crawford meet us, but he succeeded in having the money there when we were mustered out of the service.

At Junction City George Vann and Orlando Soward left us. Vann said he was going out thirty miles to his claim and when he had the cabin fit to live in he was going to send for his wife and baby. Soward was going to his parents who lived near the city. By the time we had eaten our supper and got started again it was quite dark, so we could not see much of the country, but could distinguish towns and residences by the lights. Nearly all these were on our right, so most of the settlements and towns were near the river as we were going down the north side.

When the trainman called out "Topeka" we tried to distinguish the location of our old Camp Crawford, but it was too dark and yet we could see the outline of the river. This evening when Vann left the train J. A. Studabecker took his place. He was the man whom Lieut. Stoddard bucked and gagged at Cache Creek camp for having a piece of ham taken from Capt. Pliley's tent and whom I discovered when he was nearly dead. He said he had hoped he would have a chance to express his gratitude for having him released in time to save his life. We ride together until both of us go to sleep. We had not slept any to speak of while waiting for the train at Hays City.

Wednesday, April 21, 1869

"Kansas City" was the first thing we heard this morning when the brakeman came through the car about daylight. Every one was awake instantly. After the train stopped and we had our baggage piled on the platform we did not know what to do next for we did not want to pack our baggage up to the city. Studabecker and I waited a while after bidding the boys goodbye, and then began to look for a place to store our baggage until we went to town to get new, clean clothes and take a bath and shave, so we would look more respectable. We went across to the freight house and the man in charge said we could put them in there as long as we wanted.

We then went up town and bought a complete outfit, from head to foot, from hat to shoes, and then to the bath house, and later came out fully dressed as citizens. After we had gone out on the street we met some of the other boys and we could hardly recognize each other. Some of them had full beards this morning but the razor and shears had worked wonders in their appearance, and I hardly recognized myself when I looked in a mirror. The soldier had disappeared entirely.

Studabecker is going to Paola and I am going to Olathe, so we can go together as far as Olathe. We first take a walk around the city and come to a large tent where a glassblower is making flowers out of glass besides many other designs, which were very beautiful. We stop and watch him and admire his work, when a man calls to come behind a curtain, where he shows some nice articles he has for sale, and then introduces a dice game and wants us to try our luck just for fun. We lose and win for a while and then he urges us to bet on a small sum on the table. We lose and win until we have lost about $10 when we have enough to satisfy us.

As it is only twenty-two miles to Olathe and we are several miles from the depot, we start to walk about 2 o'clock on the railroad track. We each have a revolver and shoot at a mark after we are tired walking and have rested a while. By the time we get to Shawnee it is nearly night, and we go to a farm house a short distance from the station and ask to stay till morning. We first told them we were returning soldiers on our way home. As our company was nearly all from this county we knew some of their neighbor boys, but they had not yet seen any of them. They said we could stay and they were glad to have us. They gave us the best meal we had eaten for months and treated us as the most distinguished guests. We had to give them a full history of our service, so we did not get to sleep until nearly midnight.

We heard from them about some of the boys of the company from their neighborhood. They knew Sergt. Dougherty quite well and said he was one of their best citizens and liked by everybody but he was his own worst enemy because he would drink to excess, but even then was not at all quarrelsome. He had another Indian friend, and when he began to drink he gave his money to this friend to keep for him, and he kept it too. These Indians lived in and around Shawneetown not far from the railroad station. Had we been sure Dougherty had been home we would have gone over to the railroad station, and bid him goodbye. We did not see him on the train as we came down.

Thursday, April 22, 1869

I slept in a fine bed last night, the first for over six months, and I surely enjoyed the rest after what I had gone through for several nights previous. I had a good breakfast, very much superior to any Army meal I ever ate, and the host and his good wife would not hear us mention pay for their hospitality. They asked us to call and see them whenever we passed through that way for they would certainly be very glad to see us again. We bade them goodbye and told them how well we were pleased to know them and hoped to know them better some day. They told us there would be a train going to Olathe about eight A. M., so we conclude to wait fifteen or twenty minutes and ride the rest of the way. This is the new road not yet built to Springhill, but carries passengers as far as Olathe. As this is only a signal station we had to flag the train, when it stopped and picked us up.

There were some of our company boys aboard who were going to Olathe—Dave and Lee Kitchen, John Jewell, John Atwood, A. J. Maiden, Charles Streight, Wm. Merriss, Ed. Lykins, and a few others who had enlisted in this county, and some from Paola who had enlisted under Lieut. Tilton. There were a good many got off at Shawnee Station yesterday morning among whom were Ike S. Elder and those who enlisted under him.

We arrived at Olathe about 9 o'clock where the train stopped until it returned to Kansas City, late this afternoon. Here we said our last goodbye to the boys on the train with us. I had no baggage for all I had brought from the Army, clothing, blankets and keepsakes, were still in the freight depot where I left them until I went home to Indiana which I was expecting to do in a few days. After leaving the boys I went to call on some friends I knew in town.

From them I learned that Benj. Gibson, with whom I had come from Indiana driving one of his teams, lived on my way to Springhill, so I started to walk out to his home. He had bought a farm adjoining the highway and had built a residence. The new railway was completed but a short distance beyond his farm and we could see the tracklayers at work from his house. I took dinner with Mrs. Gibson and children for he was not at home. I visited with them a couple of hours and they related a good many things that had taken place in our home town that I knew nothing about.

I finally bade them goodbye and started for Springhill on foot. There was a large force of men at work on the new road, grading and tracklaying. When last I went along here the surveyors had just passed through and left a line of stakes where the road was to be made.

It was about dark when I arrived at Mr. Corbett's and found them all at home and in good health. Of course they had to be told about my trip and all of them had a lot of questions to ask. Emma and Josie wanted to know all about the girl who had been held captive by the Indians, who she was, how old she was, and how she looked and many other questions. I learned that John Estes, John Haigler and Newt Riley arrived home yesterday and they did not know what had become of me. Corbetts had about concluded I had gone on to Indiana and would send for my trunk. They were glad that I had returned safely. They had tried to keep track of Gen. Custer's whereabouts from the papers, but no one seemed to know exactly the location of the 19th Kansas Cavalry.

From the Corbetts I learn more news from home and they also have some letters for me from my home folks. I find on my arrival that the new railroad is going through Mr. Mitchell's farm within a few feet of the big well and nothing has been done to it. The depot buildings and yards will be on a portion of what was Mr. Corbett's place and he is surveying his farm into streets, blocks and lots and will be sold out as "Corbett's Addition to Springhill."

John and his father are in the real estate business and owners of the property they are selling.

Friday, April 23, 1869

We do not hear any bugle call to get up at 4, but Mrs. Corbett calls from the foot of the stairway, "Boys, breakfast is ready," so John and I get up for breakfast. After we have eaten we go over to town for he wants me to see the improvements. Here I meet some of the boys and also many of the old neighbors. Then I go over to see Mrs. Mitchell and the family. Mr. Mitchell has gone to Chicago with a lot of cattle. His brother Rufus came in but Charlie Finch and Stoddard had not returned. They had a letter from Finch a few days ago that he was stopping at Topeka with Capt. Pliley and he was having a good time but would be home in a few days. I had determined to go back to Indiana tomorrow, so would not get to see him again.

I was with Estes and Haigler most of the day and spent the evening and night again at Corbett's. I made arrangements with John to take my trunk to Olathe in the morning where I would start to my old home. Mrs. Corbett and the girls have something to send to some of their old schoolmates and friends, so I have to pack them in my trunk. The Corbetts have treated me like a relative instead of an acquaintance and I tell them of my gratitude for their kindness. The Mitchells have been good friends and I was very sorry I did not get to see Mitchell before I left.

Saturday, April 24, 1869

We breakfast about 7 o'clock, soon after which I bid the Corbetts farewell and John takes me up to Olathe behind his favorite mule team. The train leaves at 8:45 and I just catch it and am soon on my way to Kansas City. After my arrival I find the eastern train is due to start in forty minutes and I have not time to go on to the Kansas Pacific depot after my baggage stored in the freight house unless I stay over another day, but I conclude to go on home and send for it later. I leave Kansas City at 9:50 and go over the Wabash railroad, which runs through Logansport, so will not have to change cars on the road. We did not stop to eat until we got to Galesburg, Illinois, where the train stopped first and a man came through the car yelling, "Twenty minutes for dinner" and a good many got off, and I with them. We went in and paid at the counter but before we had fairly gotten a bite the train started. Everyone jumped to his feet and ran to catch the train. I grabbed a pie off a table as I went by, which made some compensation for the money I had paid.

I had no other experiences until I arrived home in the early morning hours. So I am home again and all the family glad to see me.

So ends my diary.

FROM NO MAN'S LAND OF THE BORDER

By THEODORE F. BAYLESS

Late member of Company B, Nineteenth Kansas Volunteer
Cavalry.

THE snow storm was something fierce. Hunters
who went out for buffalo, came in for fear of
getting lost. We were out of provisions now, all
having been issued to us. The officers of my
company gave us two little cubes of sugar each. It
was the last of the officers' stores and now they would go
hungry with us. Our horses were out of feed also. Our
guides were completely bewildered and finally acknowledged
they did not know exactly where we were. A consultation
was held among the officers and they decided to send Capt.
Pliley, with sixty of the best mounted men, to find Camp
Supply, the point of our destination, and send relief as soon
as possible. When it had stopped snowing they started out
in the direction they supposed the relief to be, without anything to eat for man or beast.

Before this I went to Col. Crawford and told him I could
find the new post. He looked at me keenly and asked me if
I had ever been in this country. I told him, "No," but added, "I was raised on the frontier and am a judge of distance and direction and I can go to the new post." He
looked at my smooth face and boyish form and told me I
was too young.

"I am young," I replied, "but I am a better scout and
guide than you have in the regiment. I have been kept in
the ranks and not even allowed to go out with the

hunters and I can outshoot any of them." I informed him I
could kill more game in a day than any of them could kill
in a week. I was mad clear through and the colonel saw it.
He was an old frontiersman himself, so he just smiled and
said, "Wait until we get to Camp Supply and then come
and see me." I bid him goodbye and went through the
snow to where I should have had a tent but did not.

I think it was the 24th of November that we started out
on the march again. The snow was almost waist deep.
The horsemen led their horses and broke the way while we
footmen followed. It was very disagreeable marching. It
snowed some that day but the worst of the storm was over.
We camped near a creek that night where there was plenty
of wood and we had a good fire, but no food. I was very
hungry. I had not seen my brother for several days, so
I went over to his company. He too was hungry. I told
him about our officers giving us the last sugar they had
and he said his officers had not given them any. I was
then very sorry I had not saved some of mine for him.

That night four of us cleaned the snow off a spot several feet square and built a fire on it to dry the ground and
then made our bed on it and a tent over it with our ponchos. The ground was warm and we put in a comfortable
night except we were packed like sardines in a box and
could not turn over.

The next morning we started out through the snow
which was up to our waists in many places and although
they made a trail for us they traveled faster. Night came
on and found us still tramping through the snow and slush.
We had been two days with nothing to eat except the
sugar, and some of the boys had not that.

After dark a man came back to us and told us the camp
was about three miles ahead in a grove of timber and on a
stream supposed to be the Cimarron River, but the water

was salty. Some of the men asked me about it, and I told them as far as I had heard the Cimarron was the only stream that was salty in that part of the country. The three miles to camp seemed to me to be the longest miles I had ever traveled. Finally we came in sight of the fires and yet it seemed that we would never get to them. When we got to camp we were tired, discouraged and angry.

A small buffalo had been killed and a small portion of meat had been issued to each man. Big fires were burning and those who had gotten in early had cooked their meat, but when I tried to get to the fire to cook mine, a big fellow by the name of George Ammons shoved me away from the fire. I was in no humor to stand for such treatment and while he was a big fellow and I a boy sixteen years old, but strong and quick as a panther, I leaped upon him like a mad wildcat. I had him down in the snow and was pounding him when the lieutenant came and pulled me off. In the fracas I had lost my meat and would have gone hungry but the lieutenant took me to company quarters and gave me a larger piece. I ate my meat and being too tired to prepare a place to sleep, my bunky and I spread our ponchos on the snow, put a pair of blankets on top of them to lie on, put the others over us and went to sleep. This was our first night in Camp Starvation.

When we woke in the morning the sun was shining bright and the campfires were burning. No one was cooking breakfast, but nearly every hackberry tree was full. Our officers were in council all the forenoon and about 1 o'clock all the horsemen were called to go further. Then these horsemen were ordered to get in line of march for Camp Supply under the leadership of Capt. David L. Payne as Chief Scout.

We stayed in camp all day except a few who went hunting but I was too sore and stiff to leave camp.

The storm had driven all the game ahead of it except a few old buffalo bulls that were too slow to keep up with the herd; these were hiding in the timber near the stream.

The next day my brother, another man and myself went down the river and hunted all day. We killed a prairie dog, made a fire and cooked and ate it. We then hunted until night but found nothing. A little after sunset we heard several shots ahead of us and hurried on towards the shooting and soon came to three men who had just killed a big buffalo bull. He was in pretty good condition and they were cutting out the meat they wanted until they had all they could carry. They told us to help ourselves to all we wanted and we secured about fifty pounds apiece, all we wanted to carry to camp, which was about five miles as near as we could judge. It was now dark and our progress slow as we had to stop and rest a good many times before we reached camp.

A new danger came that I had never faced before. Wolves by the hundreds came snapping and snarling around us. We could hear them fighting over the carcass of the buffalo that we had just left. The snow was deep and it was hard for them to get anything to eat and they were very hungry and bold. We walked close together, yet the howling, barking and snarling was so great that we had to shout to each other to hear above the din. They came many times within a few feet of us and the snapping of their teeth rang out like two pieces of steel striking together. We had a hundred cartridges each and several times we thought we would have to stop and make a fight of it. We sent a shot into them occasionally when they came too close which sent them scampering away, only to return in a few minutes. Their number seemed to increase all the time.

After we had gone about three miles we met several men on their way out to see if they could find the buffalo that had been killed. The men who killed it had gotten to camp and told them where it could be found. We advised them not to go for the wolves had it all by this time. They were hungry so we gave them each a piece of meat which relieved us of a portion of our burden. As we came near camp the wolves finally left us. When we arrived in camp we turned the meat over to our company officers to be divided among the men. They gave each a piece and it was cooked without salt. We ate our meat and went to bed for we were tired out.

Maj. Dimon is the officer in command; there are several lieutenants and about three hundred men who have been left behind.

The snow melted rapidly and the weather was fine. All we had to do was our share of guard duty and try to kill something to keep from starving.

There were a good many hackberry trees on the hills around the camp and they were pretty full of berries. The fruit was sweet and the seeds could be easily crushed with the teeth. We ate them, lots of them, but they were so constipating that some of the men had to be operated on to remove the seeds. Guards had to be out to keep the hungry men from eating them.

We hunted and killed anything we could find which seemed fit to eat. One day we killed and tried to eat a raven, or carrion crow, but it was too much for us. We had better luck with a coyote for it tasted pretty good.

On the eleventh day in camp all were in a pretty bad condition. We were greatly discouraged and some openly talked of leaving camp and going out to find some way to keep from starvation. I suppose it was harder on me than it was on the older men.

It was a bright sunny day, this eleventh day in camp, and I felt as if I could not stand the hunger much longer. My brother came to get me to go hunting with him. He thought we might find some game. I told him I was not able to go. He looked at me in a strange kind of way, for he had never seen me give in before. His eyes filled with tears as he turned away, and he said, "I'll try to bring you something to eat."

I spread my blankets in the warm sunshine and laid down. I felt tired, listless and sleepy and no desire for anything, not even to live. How long I laid there I do not remember.

All at once there was cheering among the men which suddenly brought me back to consciousness. What did it mean? Was it Indians, or a rescue party? It then seemed that every man in camp was yelling. I tried to get on my feet but I was so weak it seemed as if I could not stand. Then some one cried out "Indians!" Something like an electric shock came over me and I was on my feet in an instant, carbine in hand.

Looking toward the west I saw two men coming toward our camp and three Indians following closely behind them. The white men were waving their hats and cheering. When near enough to be recognized we saw one of them was Capt. Pliley and the other, Capt. Finch of Company L. Both were cheering like mad as they waved their hats.

They were soon among us shaking hands with everybody. Some of the strongest men broke down and cried like children. Capt. Pliley's voice failed for a time so he could not speak, while the tears ran down his weather-tanned cheeks. Our officers quickly gathered around them, asking for information.

Overcoming his emotion, Capt. Pliley said, "Cheer up, men, there's plenty of grub coming back there," pointing toward the way they had come. "We found the post and we have thirteen wagons loaded with rations, but we stuck in the sand while crossing a creek a short distance back." Turning to Maj. Dimon he asked, "Have you a few men who are able and willing to go back with me to help get the wagons out of the sand?"

Twenty men were ready in an instant and anxious to go. Indeed we all felt strong after we heard that rations were so near. The good news acted like a tonic. My weakness left me; I really felt strong and my hunger almost left me.

About dark three wagons came in and a small ration was issued to each man, and that was all we were allowed to have that night. Next morning a like amount was again issued to us. We were allowed a small ration every four hours during the day and evening.

The next morning we got in line for our march to Camp Supply, bidding a glad farewell to Camp Starvation. But our memory often goes back and takes a view of the conditions as they then appeared to us. As I sit at my desk, old and gray, writing these lines, the recollection of our suffering there is burned so deep in my memory that it cannot ever be forgotten. It makes the hot blood of indignation rush through my veins when I think of the U. S. senator or congressmen from the great state of Oklahoma who are reaping and enjoying the benefits brought about by our suffering, and who refuse to vote a decent pension for the few that remain of that campaign.

"CALAMITY JANE"

—From the Collection of E. A. Brininstool.

SKETCH OF THE LIFE OF MRS. ANNA BELLE MORGAN

RS. ANNA BELLE MORGAN, wife of James S. Morgan, was captured by the Cheyenne Indians in 1868 and was recaptured by Gen. Custer in command of the 7th U. S. Cavalry and the 19th Kansas Volunteers, in March, 1869, on Elk Creek, Western Oklahoma. The subject of this sketch was Miss Anna Belle Brewster, who was born December 10, 1844, near Trenton, New Jersey. Her father and two brothers were in the War of Rebellion and members of a New Jersey regiment.

The father and one brother were killed and the other brother, Daniel Arthur Brewster, was mustered out of the service, receiving his discharge. After returning home to his mother and sister, they all moved to Pennsylvania where the mother lost her mind and died in a hospital for insane patients.

In the year 1867 Daniel left his sister with friends and went to Kansas where he took up a homestead on the Solomon River, near where the town of Delphos is now located, in Ottawa County. After he had built a cabin and prepared a suitable home he sent for his sister to come and make her home with him.

They were there only a short time when they heard the Indians were making a raid on the settlers. Women and children of the settlers were hurriedly gotten into wagons and taken to a place of safety in charge of the older men. A small band of Indians overtook them, but only tried to stampede the horses by firing guns and yelling. They frightened one team which ran away and all the Indians followed this team and the settlers reached Minneapolis, where they were safe. After the raid they all returned to their homes, where the Brewsters lived in safety.

About this time Miss Brewster made the acquaintance of a settler living a few miles distant named James S. Morgan, who was living alone on a claim. The result was that Morgan and Miss Brewster were married on the 13th day of September, 1868. They had lived in the Morgan cabin just one month when Mr. Morgan went over to the Brewster claim to finish husking corn. He had been in the habit of taking his gun with him whenever he left home, but this was a damp, foggy day, when Indians could not use their bows, so took a chance of it being perfectly safe. He did not know that the Indians had been given guns and ammunition.

Just before noon he saw three Indians come toward him and when near enough he could see their war paint, so he motioned for them to go, but they did not do so. Then he tried to get the horses loose from the wagon and while doing so, one of the Indians slipped through the corn and shot him through the hip, but did not knock him down.

The shot frightened the horses and they ran away. At the same time Morgan ran through the corn and escaped to the river near by and jumped in the water, crossing to the other side, then back again and hid in the willows.

The Indians followed the trail of drops of blood and when they saw the blood on the bank and in the water they did not follow any further and went away. After they were gone Morgan tried to stand up, but could not do so; he then crawled out through the cornfield on the prairie, where he was found by some men who were out looking for victims of the Indians' raid. They took him to Minneapolis to a hospital, where his wound received attention.

In the meantime the horses ran home, having become detached from the wagon. Mrs. Morgan, thinking her husband had met with an accident, and being a good horsewoman, jumped on one of the horses and went to look for him. When she came to the river she saw the Indians, who discovered her at the same time as they were coming toward her. She was so frightened she seemed dazed and stood still, instead of trying to escape, until they were quite near. Then she became aware of her danger and started to run away, but they soon overtook her and one of them riding alongside, hit her with a war club and knocked her off her horse, which they then caught.

After tying her so she could not struggle they bound her on her own horse, and went west for several hours. They stopped at dark and built a fire where they were later joined by several small bands of savages.

It is impossible to imagine the mental agony and physical torture endured by Mrs. Morgan during the first night of her capture. Only those who know what Indians are capable of doing, have any idea how she spent the night. In the morning they went toward the west and after several days they arrived at their main camp, on the headwaters of the Republican in the State of Colorado.

It was in this camp where Mrs. Morgan and Miss White first came together. Their captors belonged to the Cheyennes but were that portion of the tribe known as the "Dog Soldiers," being composed of the worst element of the tribe. They lived like gypsies, going from place to place, and stealing from their tribe or killing the white settlers and taking any property they could use and destroying the rest. They robbed stages, stations, stealing the horses and killing the men. They made occasional raids on the settlers, killing the men and destroying their property and mistreating the women and children, or carrying them into captivity.

The two women made several attempts to escape, but were followed and had to ride back behind their captors. The last attempt was a tramp for a night and nearly all of the next day before they were overtaken. Their feet had become so lacerated and bruised that they suffered terribly for days, so they had to submit to their life of drudgery.

It was the 15th of March, 1868, that the Dog Soldiers' camp was captured by Gen. Custer and his command of the 7th Cavalry and a portion of the 19th Kansas Volunteers, on foot. Before the circuit was complete, when the camp of the Indians was captured, they had taken the prisoners through the brush along the creek and beyond the encircling troops. It was after threatening to hang the chiefs of the tribe that the prisoners were finally delivered to the command. The troops then went across to the Washita where they were met by a supply train and continued on their march to the north to Camp Supply, to Fort Dodge and to Fort Hays. Mrs. Morgan's brother, Daniel Brewster, was present when she was recaptured and her husband met her at Fort Dodge, although not fully recovered from his wound. Together they continued to Fort Hays and then returned to their claim. Mrs. Morgan's health was not fully restored from the hardships she had endured.

The Morgans lived on their claim for many years and raised a family of one daughter and two sons, all of whom grew to maturity. Mrs. Morgan's mind became weak and finally she was sent to the Home for the Feeble Minded in Topeka where she died June 11, 1902.

Later Mr. Morgan died at the home of his daughter at Grand Junction, Colorado.

SKETCH OF THE LIFE OF SARAH C. WHITE

ARAH C. WHITE, daughter of Benjamin and Mary White, was the eldest of seven children. When her parents took up a claim in Cloud County, Kansas, she was 18 years old. Their claim was located on what was then called Granny Creek, but later was renamed White's Creek in honor of Mr. White. The year 1868 brought many settlers to northern and central Kansas who took claims on and near the Republican, Solomon and Saline Rivers. These settlers were the victims of frequent raids by the Indians, mostly Cheyennes. The U. S. troops were unable to protect them and State troops were called out for several years to assist the Regulars.

On the 13th of August, 1868, Mr. White and three sons, John, Martin and Charles, went about six miles to the river to stack some hay they had cut a few days before, leaving Mrs. White and the rest of the family at home, as they had often done before. About 10 o'clock six Indians rode up to the house and seeing no men about they dismounted and went into the house. After assuring themselves that there was no danger, they proceeded to help themselves to whatver they wanted, taking it outside. They destroyed everything they could not take by breaking furniture, cutting bedding, knocking stoves over, etc.

Two of them then seized the daughter, Sarah, and, despite her cries for help and the resistance of her frenzied mother, tied her hands and bound her on a pony.

Mrs. White and the other children were forced into the cabin while two of the Indians left with the daughter, leaving the others behind to take care of the plunder. While they were thus occupied tying it in bundles and fastening them to their ponies, Mrs. White and the children had made their escape and hid in the thick brush along the creek, where they were not discovered by the Indians.

When the Indians left, they followed the wagon trail made by Mr. White and the boys, and came in sight while they were eating their lunch. Mr. White told the boys he would walk over near where his gun was and if the Indians were friendly for them to come to him, but if they were not to jump on the horses and escape. The Indians met their father and shot him and then started toward the boys who jumped on the horses and started for the river, John on one horse and Martin and Charles on the other. One of the Indians caught John and pulled him off, or he fell off, and the Indian let him go and tried to catch the horse. John escaped in the high grass and the other two were nearly to the river when they met some other haymakers coming to their relief. They had witnessed the trouble and heard the shot. The Indians saw them coming and lost no time getting away but did not get a horse, which they wanted, to carry their plunder. Mr. White was still alive but he died shortly after and never knew of his daughter's capture.

The body was placed in the wagon and they started toward home. One of the neighbors went ahead to break the sad news to Mrs. White, but met her with the three smaller children coming to find the husband.

Couriers were sent out for volunteers to follow the Indians and in a couple of hours twenty men had assembled ready to go in pursuit. They followed the trail far into the night, but it led toward where a large Indian camp was located. After waiting several hours for reinforcements to join them they had to abandon the chase, for to attack the camp meant their defeat if not their annihilation and the death of the captive girl.

When Miss White had been taken some distance westward her captors were joined by another party, loaded with plunder, and the whole band proceeded toward the head waters of the Republican in Colorado where their principal camp was located. These Indians did not belong to the main body of Cheyennes but were what was known as the "Dog Soldiers" and consisted of the outcasts, those banished from the tribes for crimes committed on their own people. They were the thieves and robbers of their tribes and murderers of the white people of the frontier.

The worst Indians are the most superstitious, and Miss White was a Christian girl and had the Christian's assurance that she would be protected, even among thieves and robbers. When the Indians heard her talking with the "Great Spirit" they were afraid to harm her, fearing some punishment would befall them, but to have her with them would bring protection to them as well as to her.

As the weather became colder the Indians kept moving toward the south, changing their location whenever the feed for their ponies became scarce.

In March, 1869, they were camped on the North Fork of Red River and knew nothing of the approach of the 7th U. S. Cavalry and the 19th Kansas Volunteers from the south.

On March 15, 1869, Gen. Custer's command reached the North Fork of Red River and went into camp. Nearly opposite and across the river the scouts discovered where a large camp had very recently been abandoned. The next morning they took up the trail toward the northeast and that afternoon captured the camp on Elk Creek. There were over 200 lodges and 1000 Indians. Before the circuit could be completed, the two white prisoners were hurried through the brush outside the camp. As the troops had nothing to eat they let the Indians go but kept the chiefs until the tribe went on a reservation. Gen. Custer had to nearly hang the chiefs before they would bring in the white women. The command then proceeded north to Fort Hays and the captives were sent to their respective homes.

When Miss White learned that her mother and all the family had escaped, except her father, she rapidly recovered. She had believed them all killed and perhaps had died a most horrible death. In a short time she was able to do her part toward making a home in the wilderness. Being the eldest, she shared the cares of the family with her mother. She had been given a good common school education, and was fitted to give instruction to others, and so obtained a school near Clyde, Kansas. In that way she could help bear part of the financial burden of the family and clothe herself.

It was while teaching school that she became acquainted with H. C. Brooks, a farmer in the vicinity of the school house, who had been a soldier in the Civil War. Their acquaintance resulted in their marriage after the termination of her school. Her family had become self-supporting as the boys became older, so she could be spared. The White farm had become quite popular and now the Brooks farm took on new life and grew richer every year. Mr. and Mrs. Brooks were the parents of seven children, five of whom grew to maturity. Four daughters and one son are still living, as well as Mrs. Brooks who is in her seventies and has good health. Mr. Brooks died only a few years ago and Mrs. Brooks had to leave her home. Drought and hail had caused the failure of crops for several years and the income did not meet expenses and taxes.

At this writing she is living with her only son who lost his wife about two years ago. Their home is near Concordia, Cloud County, Kansas. She has filed a claim against the Government for compensation for what she had to endure at the hands of its red wards.

P. J. Phenix, a member of Company L, 19th Kansas Volunteers, has contributed much of this sketch of the life of Mrs. Brooks. He says: "Soon after I came back to Kansas, I worked five years for Miss White's uncle, Harmon Kohlman, running his saw-mill. Martin White, a brother, worked in the same mill for three years. He related to me much of the hardships his family and many others had to pass through for several years after they came to Kansas."